LEGENDS OF WARFARE

AVIATION

F-14 Tomcat

Grumman's "Top Gun" from Vietnam to the Persian Gulf

DAVID F. BROWN

SCHIFFER MILITARY
4880 Lower Valley Road • Atglen, PA 19310

Designed by Justin Watkinson
Type set in Impact/Minion Pro/Univers LT Std

ISBN: 978-0-7643-5662-9
Printed in China
5 4 3 2

Published by Schiffer Publishing, Ltd.
4880 Lower Valley Road
Atglen, PA 19310
Phone: (610) 593-1777; Fax: (610) 593-2002
E-mail: Info@schifferbooks.com
www.schifferbooks.com

For our complete selection of fine books on this and related subjects, please visit our website at www.schifferbooks.com. You may also write for a free catalog.

Schiffer Publishing's titles are available at special discounts for bulk purchases for sales promotions or premiums. Special editions, including personalized covers, corporate imprints, and excerpts, can be created in large quantities for special needs. For more information, contact the publisher.

We are always looking for people to write books on new and related subjects. If you have an idea for a book, please contact us at proposals@schifferbooks.com.

Acknowledgments

I wish to thank the following individuals who contributed to this project: Micheal Anselmo, Dave "BIO" Baranek, William Barto, Christina I. Brown, Patrick Catt, Richard Collens, Rich Cooper, Mike Crutch, Steve Czerviski, Greg A. Davis, Greg L. Davis, Dorian Dogaru, Robert F. Dorr, Paul Filmer, James Force, Andy Foster, Robert Greby, Michael Grove, Sunil Gupta, Katie Hockenluber, Takafumi Hiroe, Tony Holmes, Phillip Huston, Peter Jardim, Donald Jay, Rick Jordan, Tom Kaminski, Craig Kaston, Nicholas Kessel, Bert Kinsey, Ben Knowles, Mike Kopack, Charles Kramer, Samuel Lattuca, Bob Lawson, Ray Leader, Geoff LeBaron, Jean Francois Lipka, Tom Livesey, Roy Lock, Don Logan, Brian Marbrey, Stephen Miller, Rick Morgan, Lionel N. Paul, Ron Picciani, Jeff Puzzullo, Charles Robbins, Angelo Romano, Mick Roth, Bob Rys, Bruce Sagnor, Jared Smith, Don Spering, Keith Svendsen, Toda Toshiyuki, Henk Van Der Lugt, Theo W. Van Geffen, Wally Van Winkle, Larry Winfield, Roberto Zambon, and Michael Zwierko. This project could not have been completed without your help.

In addition, I am grateful to those who assisted me in an official capacity: Clarance F. Arnold, PH2., USN; Richard R. Burgess, William and Natalie Bell, Spike Call, CPM., USN; Bobbie Carlton, Paul Filardi, Capt., USN; Daniel G. Carpenter, TSGT., USAF; C. Curtis, PHC., USN; Russell D. Egnor, USN Photo Division; ACE Ewers, PAO, NAS Oceana; Tony Foster, PH3., USN; J. C. Frier, Jim Hampshire, PH1., USN; Nathan Laird, PMA., USN; A. LeGare, LT., USN; Mike Maus, PAO, USN; James "Gramps" McDowell, Air Operations, NAS Oceana; Daniel J. McLain, PH2., USN; George McGarry, USN; Chuck Mosely, CDR., USN; Raymond Nichols, CPO, USN; Northrop *Grumman* Corporation, Justin S. Osborne, PMA., USN; Dave "Hey Joe" Parsons, LCDR., USN; Dana Potts, Capt., USN; Milosz Reterski, PHN., USN; Richard Rodriguez, Winston E. Scott, Capt., USN; William Shayka, PH1., USN; James "Toadboy" Skarbek, LT., USN; Troy Snead, PAO, NAS Oceana; Ken Thornsley, PHC., USN; Scott Timmester, LCDR., USN; Tom Twomey, LCDR, USN; USN History Center; US Navy Safety Center and Vance Vasquez, PAO, USN.

Those of you who wish to remain anonymous: thanks, you know who you are. I apologize to anyone whom I may have inadvertently overlooked. Finally, I want to thank my wife, Christina, for always supporting me in these endeavors.

Contents

Dedicated to the memory of
ROBERT F. DORR
Friend, mentor, and colleague

"This is one of the best airplanes ever built, and it's sad to see it go away. It's just a beautiful airplane. It's powerful, it has presence, and it just looks like the ultimate fighter."

— Capt. William G. Sizemore II

Foreword

The Tomcat has touched a lot of people, including me. Although it has been more than ten years since the last Tomcat flew in the United States, it continues to capture the hearts of many people worldwide and maintains a grip on those who got close to it. The Tomcat may have been relatively large in comparison to its predecessors and contemporaries, but it was "lovely" to behold and formidable in its assigned mission, Fleet Air Defense, which necessitated the unprecedented fuel load, immense radar, and companion Phoenix long-range missile that had no equal.

The Tomcat had a tumultuous beginning at the height of the Cold War as the Navy fought to resist the pressure from the secretary of defense to develop an F-111 derivative for the Fleet Air Defense mission. That mission was crucial to protecting carrier battle groups from the regimental-sized bomber forces equipped with cruise missiles that the Soviet Union intended to use to knock out the US Navy's centerpiece of naval sea power, the aircraft carrier. The Navy had been trying to develop an airborne weapon system with long-range missiles since the late 1950s to protect the carriers. After several false starts, the technology was ready in terms of radar and missile; it just needed an interceptor to host them. Thus was born a lovely fighter, the Tomcat.

My quest to be a part of the Tomcat community started after seeing the first images of the developmental aircraft in *Aviation Week* while I was in the midst of finishing high school. I was following the development of the Tomcat closely as I entered college. It looked amazing and deadly with those twin tails and sleek lines. The Marine Corps was still in the Tomcat program at that time and used a photo of a Tomcat to induce prospective aviators to sign on the dotted line. I did exactly that as a freshman in college and headed to Quantico shortly after that in my quest to get in the cockpit of one. When the Marines opted out of the Tomcat as a replacement for the venerable Phantom as the first Marines were training at VF-124, I was still smitten, as Ernest Hemingway stated so eloquently. I was fortunate enough to land in the Pentagon after my commissioning and Quantico "finishing school" experience, and I ended up sharing an office with a Tomcat pilot who suggested I consider an interservice transfer if I truly wanted to pursue my quest. Two years later I arrived at Naval Air Station Oceana in Virginia Beach, wearing wings of gold on my Navy uniform with orders to Fighter Squadron 101, the "Grim Reapers," where I would begin my training as part of the Tomcat community. I could hardly withhold my excitement.

It's now been twenty-five years since my last flight in a Tomcat, which put me over 2,000 hours and 700 carrier-arrested landings in the Tomcat. I am still smitten with the big fighter that was such a leap ahead in technology at the time of introduction.

Midway through my career in the Tomcat, I was fortunate enough to meet David F. Brown. That was thirty years ago, in 1987, when he was working on his proposed book, *Tomcats Forever*, with the late Bob Dorr. They heard I had amassed a collection of images from my time as a VF-102 "Diamondback" from 1981 to 1986, and they came to visit. I never flew without a camera loaded with color film, and I left the "Diamondbacks" in 1986, with over 1,500 hours and easily that number of images. After pursuing my collection of imagery, they selected one of my images for the cover, thereby beginning our collective friendship and collaboration ever since. I was a bit surprised when Bob Dorr kept remarking about Bureau Numbers (BuNos) and trying to see if my images of Phantoms had the resolution to discern specific aircraft. His quest was to amass an image of every Phantom that ever flew, and Dave's quest was to do the same for the Tomcat. I noted that for future opportunities to take pictures.

Our professional and personal connection continued over the succeeding years, and I remembered his quest when taking pictures and returning to the community for another operational tour. When he announced he intended to produce a book on the Tomcat that focused on a literal roll call, Bureau Number by Bureau Number, it was no surprise to me. That effort, *Tomcat Alley*, has become a must-have of any serious enthusiast's collection. Assembling and cataloging the images was no easy task. He was relentless in this endeavor and became known as "Mr. Tomcat" due to his faithfulness and diligence in visiting NAS Oceana and cataloging every Tomcat he saw. He was trusted by Base Operations, who gave him access to the ramp, flight line, and shooting locations alongside the active runways. His very favorite spot became known as "Dave's Ditch," from where he got spectacular images of takeoffs and landings of his favorite fighter. When Tomcat squadrons returned from deployment, Dave was there.

There were special Tomcats to Dave that he tracked relentlessly. When the Tomcats began reaching the end of their service life, and the SARDIP program began dismantling aircraft slated for disposal, Dave was there. Their last "close-ups" before destruction were by Dave. Then came BuNo 159610, an F-14A that had been remanufactured into a D model. It was very special indeed, having shot down a Libyan MiG-23 in January 1989 while serving with VF-32. Due to its unique history, the National Air and Space Museum had requested it for display as part of the national collection housed at Udvar-Hazy. Dave was very aware of that, and when he arrived at Oceana one fine day, it was already in the process of being dismantled. If Dave had not been there, it would have been stripped before being ground into pieces no bigger than five inches; an ignoble and undeserved end to a very special Tomcat. But Dave was there, and he raised the alarm. Apparently, the list of F-14A models to be saved for museum or static display did not take into account A models remanufactured into D models; hence the error. But Dave was there, and his raising of the alarm spurred the Chief of Naval Operations and F-14 Program Office into action to reconstitute F-14D (R), 159610, thereby saving it from extinction. When it was displayed to the public following the Tomcat Sunset of November 2006, Dave was there.

When a request for the history of a specific Bureau Number comes from a museum or individual, Dave is there with the most extensive library of images and related history. He has truly earned his title of "Mr. Tomcat." The entire community of aircrew, maintainers, industry partners, and enthusiasts owe him a huge debt of thanks for his exhaustive efforts to preserve the legacy of the F-14 Tomcat. Let me be the first to say thank you from all of us!

Dave Parsons
"Hey Joe"
2,000+ hours in the F-14A/B Tomcat

CHAPTER 1

TFX vs. VFX

F-111B, BuNo 151973, was the fourth example manufactured by Grumman. Of interest were the Phoenix Missiles mounted on pylons that swiveled during wing-swept movement, thereby keeping ordnance parallel to the fuselage and reducing drag. Unfortunately, this mechanism added even more weight to an already overweight airframe. This example was written off on April 21, 1967, following compressor stalls in both engines during takeoff. Test pilots Charles Wangman and Ralph Donnell perished in the crash. *Grumman*

The Tactical Fighter Experimental Program (TFX) was a result of a US Air Force requirement for a successor to the Republic F-105 Thunderchief. Initially, the program was known as the TFX/F-111 Project. On February 14, 1961, Defense Secretary Robert McNamara decreed that TFX would become a joint Air Force–Navy program. He viewed his decision as a cost-effective way of acquiring a jack-of-all-trades fighter/attack aircraft capable of meeting the US Air Force's requirement for a high-speed, low-level fighter/attack aircraft, and the US Navy's desire for a long-range interceptor capable of defending carrier battle groups from the growing threat posed by Soviet bomber- and submarine-launched antiship missiles. From the outset, the Navy opposed TFX, citing compromises required to accommodate the Air Force's requirement for its low-level attack mission. On October 1, 1961, both services issued requests for proposals (RFPs) to Lockheed, North American, Boeing, and teams consisting of Republic / Chance Vought, General Dynamics / Grumman and McDonnell Douglas. General Dynamics / Grumman won the TFX contract, beating out Boeing during very contentious and lengthy bidding and rebidding process.

General Dynamics, the manufacturer of the F-111A, collaborated with Grumman to produce the navalized version designated the F-111B. General Dynamics chose Grumman because of Grumman's long and storied history of building fighter aircraft for the US Navy. Two variants, F-111A and F-111B, were thought to be the best solution to meet the needs of both services. The first Grumman constructed, F-111B, BuNo 151970, flew from their Calverton Test Facility on May 18, 1965. It became apparent once test flights commenced October 1965 that at nearly 78,000 pounds, the F-111B was too heavy to conduct safe operations from the deck of an aircraft carrier, and it was severely underpowered, resulting in dangerous engine compressor stalls. General Dynamics

The Pratt & Whitney TF30 was the world's first production turbofan with afterburner. The non-afterburner version was used in early A-7 Corsair IIs. This example with afterburner was the type selected for use in the F-111. The first five F-111Bs (151970-4) were fitted with TF30-P-1; the last two (152714-5) had the P-12. The power plant was susceptible to compressor stalls even after being adapted for use to power the F-14A. *US Navy*

Grumman design 303-60 initially featured a single vertical stabilizer. A series of modifications based on wind tunnel testing and in-depth design studies resulted in designs 303A through 303E. The latter design, incorporating twin vertical stabilizers, became the design we recognize as the F-14 Tomcat. *Grumman*

and Grumman attempted to solve the weight issue with a Super Weight Improvement Program (SWIP), commencing with the fourth F-111B (BuNo 151973), the first example equipped with an escape capsule instead of ejection seats. Unfortunately, the addition of the escape capsule more than offset the weight reductions achieved by SWIP. SWIP was in turn followed by the CWIP, the Colossal Weight Improvement Program. While SWIP was designed to trim weight inter-

The X-5 and XF10F were prototypes using variable-sweep wing technology based on technical data gleaned from a World War II German design, the P.1101. This aircraft, XF10F, 124435, was the sole example of the type to fly. It was grossly underpowered and challenging to fly. The program was canceled in 1953. *Grumman*

nally, CWIP called for external and additional internal weight-saving modifications. Despite two attempts at weight reduction, the F-111B was still too heavy for safe arrested landings and catapult launches from carrier decks.

Following a myriad of problems, including a pair of fatal crashes, the F-111B program was canceled on March 4, 1968. During Senate Armed Service Committee testimony, VAdm. Thomas Connolly, the director of Naval Air Warfare, Office of the Chief of Naval Operations, had this to say about the F-111B: "All the thrust in Christendom couldn't make a fighter out of this airplane." Congress agreed and stripped the funding from the F-111B program, effectively ending it.

Even before the cancellation of the F-111B, Grumman was trying to interest the Navy in a new design utilizing variable-geometry wings, twin Pratt and Whitney TF30 power plants, two-man crews, the Hughes AWG-9 radar, and the Phoenix missile system. The new design was basically a lighter, streamlined version of the F-111B and was in line with a NAVAIR request for proposals for the Naval Fighter Experimental or VFX program. With knowledge gained from the construction of its swing-wing fighter and the XF10F Jaguar and experience gained from the TFX/F-111B program, work on just such a fighter aircraft, Grumman design 303-60, was already well underway at company expense. Ultimately, it would beat the McDonnell Douglas submission and be awarded the VFX contract on February 3, 1969. The design would become known as the F-14.

CHAPTER 2

Drawing Board to First Flight

Tomcat No. 1, BuNo 157980, photographed undergoing construction on the shop floor at Grumman's facility in Calverton, Long Island, New York. It would be the first of 712 Tomcats to roll down this assembly line, 632 for the US Navy and eighty for the Imperial Iranian Air Force. *Grumman*

To speed up the process of fielding the next-generation Navy fighter and to avoid interference from Defense Secretary McNamara, Grumman and the Navy skipped the prototype phase, moving directly to the manufacture of preproduction aircraft. Late in 1970, a full month ahead of schedule and fewer than two years after the contract signing, Grumman was ready to begin test flights of the F-14. On December 21, 1970, following months of ground tests, Tomcat No. 1 was prepared for its first test flight. Chief test pilot Robert Smyth was at the controls, with project test pilot William Miller occupying the back seat. Late that afternoon, 157980 lifted off from the Calverton runway. Due to impending darkness, Smythe opted for a short flight consisting of two low-speed circuits of the field. The wings were fixed in the forward-swept configuration, the landing gear was pinned down, and the aircraft was carrying four inert AIM-7 Sparrow missiles. This flight was made to satisfy a contract requirement. Additional, in-depth testing would commence after the Christmas holiday.

The second flight took place on December 30, 1970. The crew of Smythe and Miller switched seats for this flight. At 1018, 157980 lifted off from the Calverton runway with Miller at the controls. Escorted by a pair of chase planes, the flight proceeded across the Long Island Sound. Approximately thirty minutes later, a chase plane pilot spotted a trail of hydraulic fluid coming from the Tomcat. At about the same time, Miller reported a failure of the primary hydraulic system and immediately turned back toward Calverton. The Tomcat was designed with triple-redundant flight control systems; Primary, Secondary, and Combat Survival. Miller

and Smythe blew down the landing gear with the emergency nitrogen system while they were 4 miles from the Calverton runway, then the secondary hydraulic system failed. The Combat Survival System, consisting of an electric pump used to move only the rudders and horizontal stabilizers, was then engaged. Nearing the threshold of Calverton's runway, the Combat Survival System started to show signs of failure. Smythe ejected first, followed a half second later by Miller. Both escaped low-level ejections with minor injuries and were able to carry on as Grumman test pilots.

At the time of the crash of 157980, twelve preproduction Tomcats were nearing flight worthiness or were under construction. Each was assigned and equipped for a specific test regime. For example, 157980, Tomcat No. 1, was to be utilized for expanding the F-14's flight envelope and high-speed tests. Its loss presented a dilemma for Grumman engineers because the first twelve Tomcats were already fitted with or scheduled to be equipped with mission-specific test equipment. This resulted in the first preproduction Tomcat being replaced in the test regime by No. 12, the last preproduction Tomcat, 157991. Grumman designated it 1X. Besides the discovery of the issue of hydraulic-line fatigue, one other important aspect of the Tomcat's construction was discovered during the investigation of the crash: the strength of its wing box or box beam.

General Dynamics had relied on a bolted-up, steel wing box for its swept-wing mechanism. Grumman opted for an all-titanium box beam constructed by utilizing a pioneering technique known as electron-beam welding. This process resulted in higher strength and a weight savings of 900 pounds. When the box beam of 157980

F-14A, 157980, on its ill-fated second flight. It crashed while on final approach to Calverton, following a complete failure of its redundant hydraulic systems. A follow-up investigation indicated hydraulic-line fatigue resulted in the failure of the flight control systems. *Grumman*

The next preproduction Tomcat, 157981, did not fly until May 24, 1971. It was used to explore slow-speed handling. Next in line was 157991(1X), with the first flight on August 31, 1971, taking over the high-speed-handling test regime of 157980. These were followed by 157983, October 26, 1971; 157984, November 26, 1971; 157985, December 10, 1971; 157982 and 157988, December 28, 1971; 157987, December 31, 1971; 157989, February 29, 1972; 157990, March 6, 1972; and 157986, September 12, 1973 (see the preproduction chart for details).

was retrieved from the crash site, having been dug out from a depth of 6 feet, it was discovered to have suffered very little damage from the impact. It was further testament to the strength of aircraft manufactured by the Grumman Iron Works.

Right-side wing attachment point for the Grumman electron-beam welded titanium box beam. The box beam was so strong that one of the two wing attachment points could fail without causing the destruction of the wing. *Author*

F-14A, 157981, conducting in-flight refueling tests with Grumman A-6A, 148617. This preproduction Tomcat was utilized for low-speed handling tests until May 13, 1974, when it suffered an in-flight APU fire. The aircrew landed safely, but the aircraft was written off. *Grumman*

THE FIRST TWELVE PRE-PRODUCTION F-14 TOMCATS

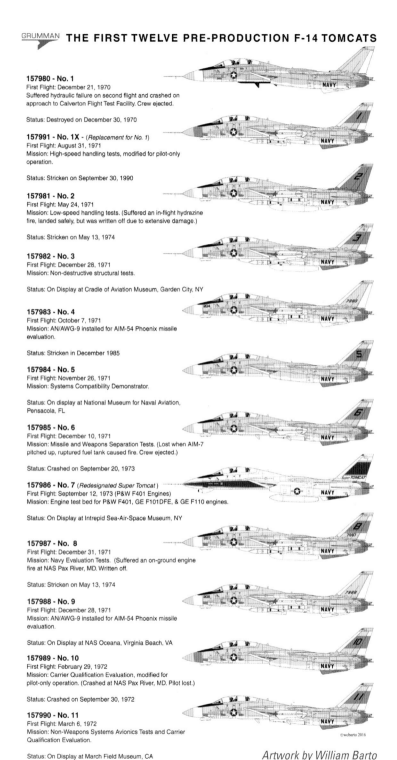

157980 - No. 1
First Flight: December 21, 1970
Suffered hydraulic failure on second flight and crashed on approach to Calverton Flight Test Facility. Crew ejected.

Status: Destroyed on December 30, 1970

157991 - No. 1X - (Replacement for No. 1)
First Flight: August 31, 1971
Mission: High-speed handling tests, modified for pilot-only operation.

Status: Stricken on September 30, 1990

157981 - No. 2
First Flight: May 24, 1971
Mission: Low-speed handling tests. (Suffered an in-flight hydrazine fire, landed safely, but was written off due to extensive damage.)

Status: Stricken on May 13, 1974

157982 - No. 3
First Flight: December 28, 1971
Mission: Non-destructive structural tests.

Status: On Display at Cradle of Aviation Museum, Garden City, NY

157983 - No. 4
First Flight: October 7, 1971
Mission: AN/AWG-9 installed for AIM-54 Phoenix missile evaluation.

Status: Stricken in December 1985

157984 - No. 5
First Flight: November 26, 1971
Mission: Systems Compatibility Demonstrator.

Status: On display at National Museum for Naval Aviation, Pensacola, FL

157985 - No. 6
First Flight: December 10, 1971
Mission: Missile and Weapons Separation Tests. (Lost when AIM-7 pitched up, ruptured fuel tank caused fire. Crew ejected.)

Status: Crashed on September 20, 1973

157986 - No. 7 (Redesignated Super Tomcat)
First Flight: September 12, 1973 (P&W F401 Engines)
Mission: Engine test bed for P&W F401, GE F101DFE, & GE F110 engines.

Status: On Display at Intrepid Sea-Air-Space Museum, NY

157987 - No. 8
First Flight: December 31, 1971
Mission: Navy Evaluation Tests. (Suffered an on-ground engine fire at NAS Pax River, MD. Written off.)

Status: Stricken on May 13, 1974

157988 - No. 9
First Flight: December 28, 1971
Mission: AN/AWG-9 installed for AIM-54 Phoenix missile evaluation.

Status: On Display at NAS Oceana, Virginia Beach, VA

157989 - No. 10
First Flight: February 29, 1972
Mission: Carrier Qualification Evaluation, modified for pilot-only operation. (Crashed at NAS Pax River, MD. Pilot lost.)

Status: Crashed on September 30, 1972

157990 - No. 11
First Flight: March 6, 1972
Mission: Non-Weapons Systems Avionics Tests and Carrier Qualification Evaluation.

Status: On Display at March Field Museum, CA

©wcbarto 2016

Artwork by William Barto

F-14A, 157982, was used for nondestructive structural tests. It is viewed here in flight with four inert AIM-54 Phoenix missiles. Of interest are the early-style external fuel tanks. Tomcat No. 3 was acquired by the Cradle of Aviation Museum in 1995. *Grumman*

F-14A, 157983, had the AN/AWG-9 installed for AIM-54 Phoenix missile tests and evaluations. This airframe was delivered to AMARC October 27, 1981, and was coded AN1K0004. It departed the boneyard on August 5, 1985, and was sent to NATTC Memphis, Tennessee. *Author's collection*

Preproduction Tomcats 157988(9), 157984(5), and 157985(6) photographed circa 1972 at NAS Point Mugu, California. BuNo 157985 was written off on June 20, 1973, when an AIM-7 Sparrow pitched up, rupturing a fuel tank. The crew consisted of Samuel M. "Pete" Purvis and William G. "Tank" Sherman, both of whom ejected. *Grumman via Craig Kaston*

F-14A, 157986, flew for the first time on September 9, 1973, and was powered by a pair of P&W F401-PW-400 engines. This power plant proved to be an unsatisfactory replacement for the TF30. The airframe was used to test various engines, including the GE F101DFE and GE F110-GE-400. It was photographed in "Super Tomcat" markings undergoing F-14D Pre-deployment Update flight tests near NATC Patuxent River. *Grumman*

F-14A, 157987, photographed April 22, 1974, at NATC Patuxent River, Maryland. It was utilized for Navy evaluation tests. This Tomcat was written off on May 13, 1974, following an on-the-ground engine fire. *Author's collection*

F-14A, 157989, was modified for pilot-only flight and was utilized for carrier qualifications. Grumman test pilot Bob Miller lost his life in this Tomcat when it crashed into the Chesapeake Bay on June 30, 1972, while practicing for an air show. *Picciani*

F-14A, 157990, was initially assigned to Point Mugu for systems compatibility tests. It is seen here taking part in carrier qualification evaluation. It is currently preserved and displayed on March Field Air Museum in fictitious VF-1 markings. *US Navy*

F-14A, 157991, preproduction Tomcat 1X was used to test the high-speed handling characteristics of the F-14. Of interest is the single crew member. This airframe was modified for pilot-only flight. It was bailed to NASA for spin and high-angle-of-attack tests. *Spering*

In addition to the first twelve preproduction Tomcats, eight production Tomcats—158612, 158613, 158614, 158615, 158616, 158617, 158618, and 158619—were utilized for testing at NATC Patuxent River, NATF Lakehurst, Pacific Missile Test Center, NAS Point Mugu, and Naval Weapons Center, China Lake.

Grumman adopted this patch to represent the F-14 Tomcat. Grumman artist Dick Milligan designed it. The twin-tail configuration of the first design was retained. *Author*

Early Tomcat patch created by Grumman artist Jim Rodriquez. This design was not adopted by Grumman. Of interest is the inclusion of twin tails, a trademark of future Tomcat patches. *Author*

F-14A, 158616, was an example of Block 60 production Tomcat pressed into service for test and evaluation. This Tomcat performed carrier suitability testing following the June 30, 1972, crash of No. 10, 157989. On May 16, 1980, it became the second F-14 sent to AMARC. It departed AMARC on October 15, 1985, was remanufactured to Block 135 status, and was assigned to VF-201. *Spering*

CHAPTER 3
RAGs to Readiness: The First Tomcats Arrive

F-14A, 158637, assigned to Fleet Replacement Squadron (FRS) VF-124, photographed during September 1974 at NAS Miramar, California. This cat used all its nine lives, surviving until January 6, 2004, when it was SARDIPed at NAS Norfolk. *Spering*

In December 1973, the first USMC flight crews reported to VF-124 for Tomcat training. At the time it was thought that the Marines would transition to the Tomcat from the F-4 Phantom II. Instead, the USMC opted to update their fleet of Phantoms. Departing Marine crews were replaced by the arrival of Iranian aircrews. *Catt*

The first Tomcat training or readiness squadron, VF-124, known as the "Gunfighters," was assigned to the Pacific Fleet at NAS Miramar and received its first F-14A Tomcat on October 18, 1972. BuNo 158617 was transferred to VF-124 from the Pacific Missile Test Center on a temporary basis. By year's end, 28.1 flight hours were logged in this aircraft. It was also put to good use by VF-124's FRAMP Department to train maintainers. The first two operational fleet squadrons, VF-1 (the "Wolfpack") and VF-2 (the "Bounty Hunters") stood up on October 14, 1972. Training for both squadrons was conducted until they both were chopped from VF-124 on July 1, 1973. In addition to training the first two Pacific Fleet Tomcat squadrons, VF-124 also trained the first two Atlantic Fleet Tomcat squadrons, the "Tophatters" of VF-14 and the "Swordsmen" VF-32.

On June 23, 1975, the Chief of Naval Operations directed the establishment of an East Coast F-14 Fleet Replacement Squadron as a component of the current F-4 Phantom II FRS, VF-101 (the "Grim Reapers"). The first F-14A to be assigned was BuNo 159428, arriving on December 18, 1975. VF-84 (the "Jolly Rogers") and the "Black Aces" of VF-41 were the first two Atlantic Fleet squadrons transitioned to the Tomcat by VF-101 with training commencing during March 1976. The typical Tomcat training syllabus consisted of

two days of firefighting school,

one week of survival, evasion, resistance, and escape school,

two days of aviation physiology / water survival,

two weeks of instrument school,

six weeks of familiarization school (FAM),

five weeks of basic employment of the AWG-9 radar,

two weeks of weapons employment,

five weeks of air combat maneuvering (ACM),

four weeks of advanced employment (threat tactics and intercepts), and

four Weeks of carrier qualifications (CQ), day and night.

The training pipeline was now flowing, providing Tomcat pilots, radar intercept officers (RIOs) and maintainers, to the fleet. The primary mission of both Fleet Replacement squadrons was to "provide the fleet with replacement Pilots and Radar Intercept Officers, who are qualified in the F-14A Tomcat in accordance with the Chief of Naval Operations (CNO) approved syllabus," continued right up until VF-124 was disestablished, and VF-101 was deactivated.

F-14, 160406, assigned to the "Grim Reapers" of VF-101, successfully recovers or "traps" aboard the USS *Independence* (CV-62) on June 7, 1979. Carrier qualifications were and still are the most challenging part of the Navy's flight-training syllabus regardless of the aircraft flown. *US Navy*

CHAPTER 4
The A, B, C, and Ds of the Tomcat

The first production Tomcat, 158612, was photographed fresh from the Grumman factory at Dulles IAP on May 20, 1972. The number "13" is the Grumman-applied shop number, signifying this is the thirteenth Tomcat constructed. Initially used for electromagnetic-compatibility tests, it was then remanufactured to Block 135 standards before being reissued to VF-201. It was later assigned to VF-41 and saw combat during the opening stages of OEF, making it the oldest active Tomcat in the fleet. *Author's collection*

F-14A

The first production Tomcat to roll down the Grumman assembly lines received the designation F-14A. A total of 478 were delivered to the US Navy, and an additional seventy-nine were delivered to the Imperial Iranian Air Force. The last Iranian Tomcat, BuNo 160378, was embargoed following the Iranian Revolution and was later pressed into service with the US Navy. The F-14A was initially powered by the Pratt and Whitney TF-30-P-412. These engines produced enough thrust for a maximum speed of Mach 2.4 and a rate of climb of 30,000 feet per minute. The final 102 F-14As were fitted with the more reliable Pratt and Whitney TF30-P-414A. At the heart of the Tomcat was the Hughes AWG-9 Pulse-Doppler, a multimode radar capable of tracking twenty-four hostile aircraft and cruise missiles as it computes fire-control solutions for six targets simultaneously at ranges exceeding 100 miles. A "core" group of F-14As were later fitted with the upgraded Countermeasure, Warning, and Control System, AN/ALR-67, the AAQ-14 and AAQ-25 LANTIRN pod and Programmable Tactical Information Display (PTID). Select F-14A/B models and all F-14Ds assumed the reconnaissance mission via the TARPS pod. This system was later updated to a TARPS Digital Imaging System. F-14As soldiered on to the very end. The last operational Tomcat squadron, VF-211, flew their remaining A models to AMARC on September 12, 2004.

F-14A+, F-14A(PLUS), F-14B, F-14B(UPGRADE)

The F-14A+ or F-14A(PLUS) began full-scale production in March 1987. The first example, 162910, was initially used in the F-14A+

test program before its delivery to the Navy on November 1, 1987. A total of thirty-eight new-build examples followed at a rate of approximately two per month. The final new-build F-14A+, 163411, was delivered on February 20, 1990. A further forty-eight F-14A+ Tomcats were added by upgrading F-14As. Upgrades were carried out at three locations: Grumman Calverton, NADEP Norfolk, and Grumman St. Augustine, Florida. Major improvements incorporated the significantly more powerful General Electric F110-GE-400 engines, replacing the Pratt and Whitney TF30s, which were susceptible to compressor stalls. The GE engines also allowed for carrier launches without the use of afterburner. Other improvements included Engine Fatigue Monitoring System, ALR-67 Threat Warning & Recognition System, DLC/APC or Direct Lift Control/Approach Power Control MOD, AN/AWG-15 Fire Control System, ARC-182 Have Quick UHF/VHF radio, and improved gun gas purge system. On May 1, 1991, the designation was changed to F-14B. Sixty-seven F-14Bs received additional upgrades designed to extend their service life to 7,000 hours and improve their combat effectiveness and survivability. These improvements included relocation of the ALR-67 RHAW's forward antenna, rewiring to allow carriage of the ALQ-167 ECM pod, LAU-138 AIM-9 launcher with chaff and flare dispensing capability, rewiring for MIL-STD-1553 armament, avionics and electronic warfare data buses fitted with PTID, AYK-14 Mission Computer (FMC), and AWG-15H, making the F-14B(UPGRADE) capable of launching GPS-dependent weapons such as the GBU-31/32 JDAM and AGM-154 JSOW. These received the designation F-14B(UPGRADE). Because there was insufficient room in the rear cockpit for a LANTIRN control panel (CP) and the TARPS recon control panel (RCP), squadrons tended to maintain a cadre

F-14B, 163220, assigned to VF-143, is an example of an F-14B(UPGRADE). It was photographed on October 21, 2004. The orange pod is a Tactical Aircrew Combat Training System (TACTS) pod used to monitor air combat training. Mounted below the TACTS pod is the LANTIRN pod. *Author*

Every inch a Super Tomcat, preproduction Tomcat No. 7, complete with General Electric F110 engines, was photographed taking part in the F-14D Pre-deployment Update flight test program. These tests were flown from NATC Patuxent River. Of interest are the pair of HARM missiles, four Mk. 84 (2,000 lb.) bombs, two AIM-9 Sidewinders, and external fuel tanks. *Grumman*

of dedicated TARPS aircraft. The rest were fitted for LANTIRN and night vision goggles (NVGs). TARPS-DI was not part of the UPGRADE package. Instead, it was retrofitted to select TARPS aircraft. All F-14B(UPGRADE) Tomcats retained the Link-4 Data Link system, updated in late 1990, with the ASW-27C Fighter-to-Fighter Datalink 17.

F-14B

(Not That F-14B; the Other One)

The F-14A was always thought of as a provisional design in search of a more powerful and reliable power plant to match the airframe. Preproduction F-14A, BuNo 157986, was designated as the engine test Tomcat for the Pratt & Whitney F401-P400 engines. Its maiden flight with the F401 took place on September 9, 1973. Following flight evaluations totaling thirty-three hours, the airframe, then designated F-14B, was put in storage at Calverton.

Early in 1981, 157986 was fitted with a pair of General Electric F101DFE, Derivative Fighter Engines. With 65,000 total pounds of thrust, the F101DFE produced sufficient thrust to accelerate the resurrected F-14B from Mach 0.8 to Mach 1.8 in only ninety seconds. More importantly, with a thrust-to-weight ratio of approximately 1:1, the F-14B could be catapulted from a carrier deck without the use of afterburner. Despite the success of these trials, the Navy opted to cancel this test program in September 1981. Preproduction Tomcat No. 7 headed back to storage, but not for long. During July 1984, yet another engine variant was

installed for testing: the General Electric F110-GE-400. Around this time, 157986 picked up the moniker "Super Tomcat." Additional testing confirmed the F110-GE-400 was the power plant / airframe match Grumman was searching for. By November 1987, production F-14A+ models were rolling off the Grumman assembly line. The type was later redesignated F-14B in May 1991.

F-14C

The F-14C was a proposed variant of the F-14B, with enhanced avionics making it more multimission capable. No F-14Cs were manufactured.

F-14D, F-14D(R)

The F-14D, often referred to as the true Super Tomcat, was the final variant of the Tomcat. Similar in outward appearance to an F-14B, the D model incorporated the same GE F110-GE-400 engines, but similarities stopped there. The Super Tomcat was equipped with the improved AN/APG-71 radar, Joint Tactical Information Distribution System (JTIDS), Airborne Self Protection Jammer (ASPJ), a glass cockpit, Infra-Red Search and Track (IRST), and NACES, the Naval Aircrew Common Ejection Seats. A total of thirty-seven new-build F-14Ds were delivered, starting with 163412 on May 23, 1990. The last new-built F-14D, 164604, was delivered on July 10, 1992. Eighteen F-14As were remanufactured and designated F-14D(R). These were Bureau Numbers 159592, 159595, 159600, 159603, 159610, 159613, 159618, 159619, 159628,

Super Tomcat 21. *Grumman*

Super Tomcat 21. *Grumman*

F-14D(R), 159619, assigned to VF-31 and photographed March 11, 2006, one day after the Tomcat's final cruise, a combat cruise to the Mediterranean Sea and the Persian Gulf. This Tomcat was initially delivered to the Navy as an F-14A on October 27, 1975. During the early 1990s, it was withdrawn from service and upgraded, becoming the ninth F-14A upgraded to F-14D standards. This particular example is currently on display at the Florida Air Museum, Lakeland, Florida. *Author*

159629, 159630, 159633, 159635, 161154, 161158, 161159, 161163, and 161166.

Quick Strike, AST21 and ASF-14 Super Tomcat 21

The Super Tomcat 21 was Grumman's proposed answer to the need for a quick-strike or advanced-strike fighter (ASF). Had it been built, It would have looked like a highly modified F-14D, featuring GE-F110-129 power plants with thrust vectoring allowing the Tomcat to achieve Mach 1+ supercruise without the use of afterburner.

Other design features would have included enlarged control surfaces, leading-edge root extensions enhancing low-speed capabilities, and additional fuel, all controlled by a digital flight control system. The heart of the Tomcat's weapons system, the APG-71 radar, would have been significantly modified. Upgrades to the cockpit, HUD, and mission computers were also proposed.

Thought to be too expensive, the ASF-14 or Super Tomcat 21 was not built. The Navy instead opted for the F/A-18E/F/G. But imagine a Super Tomcat 21 crammed with digital electronics, capable of hauling more ordnance farther and faster and delivering it on target with the same or better accuracy as a Super Hornet.

CHAPTER 5
Peeping Tom

Although initially developed and fielded as a "Fleet Defender," with the introduction of TARPS (Tactical Airborne Reconnaissance Pod System), the Tomcat matured into a capable Tactical Reconnaissance platform. All F-14D models were wired for TARPS. Select F-14As and F-14Bs were also modified for TARPS. In the case of the F-14A/B, standard practice involved assigning three TARPS aircraft to one squadron per carrier air wing. The system consisted of a 17-foot-long pod weighing 1,850 pounds, mounted under the fuselage on the starboard side between the engines (right rear Phoenix station). The pod's three camera bays were controlled by the radar intercept officer (RIO). Each bay held specific cameras for specific tasks. The aft bay contained an AN/AAD-5 Infrared Line Scanner Camera for night missions, day missions, and mission trace. The front bay held a KS-87, a 6-inch-focal-length camera on a rotating mount capable of pointing straight down or at a 45-degree angle. The middle bay held a 9-inch-focal-length KA-99 Panoramic Camera capable of rotating horizon to horizon and loaded with 1,000 feet of film, each frame measuring 9 x 36 inches. The high-altitude KA-93 and, later, the KS-153 were interchangeable with the KA-99. Late in their service life, the pods received digital imagery (DI) and electro-optical (OI) improvements. The Pullnix digital camera was installed in the pod's forward bay, replacing the wet-film KS-87 camera. Digital images were then sent via the Tomcat's UHF radio. The first squadron to deploy the TARPS-DI was VF-32. The new system was validated over Bosnia when a VF-32 Tomcat transmitted near-real-time digital imagery to an F-15E Strike Eagle via E-2 Hawkeye during a simulated strike. The final improvement to TARPS was the TARPS-CD, which incorporated a transmitter and was entirely digital.

Two reinforced concrete aircraft hangars at the Ahmed Al Jaber Airfield show the results of a coalition bombing strike during Operation Desert Storm. The photograph was taken by a Fighter Squadron 84 (VF-84) F-14A Tomcat aircraft using the Tactical Air Reconnaissance Pod System (TARPS). *Navy*

F-14A, 160696, hauling a TARPS pod and a pair of inert CATM-7 Sparrows utilized as counterweights to maintain the Tomcat's center of gravity. Of interest in this shot are the extended wing glove vanes that automatically deployed at supersonic speeds. Designed to increase the wing area, the glove vanes were later rendered inoperable in F-14A models and deleted in the much-improved F-14B/D models. *Grumman*

TARPS mounted on station 5 on an F-14B assigned to VF-103, the "Jolly Rogers." This configuration required the carriage of forward Phoenix pallets or inert AIM-7s as ballast to maintain the center of gravity. At 17 feet in length and 1,850 pounds, TARPS was the largest device carried by the Tomcat. *Author*

CHAPTER 6
Tomcat to Bombcat

Throughout the 1980s, the Tomcat community continued air-to-ground ordnance trials with test-and-evaluation operational squadrons, but at a slow pace. Both Tomcat Fleet Replacement squadrons, VF-124, and VF-101, incorporated lessons learned from these trials to develop a training syllabus to turn Tomcat crews into Bombcat crews. Tomcat squadrons on both coasts soon became proficient dropping the Mk. 80 series of "dumb" bombs with consistently good results. *Grumman*

The Tomcat was designed from the outset to deliver air-to-ground ordnance. During 1973, to attract foreign customers, preproduction Tomcat 157990 was flown with fourteen Mk. 82 500-pound inert bombs hung on modified hardpoints.

With the cancellation of the A-12, looming budget cuts, and the impending retirement of the Grumman A-6 Intruder, the Tomcat was called upon to fill the gap. In 1993, Lockheed Martin proposed a modified version of their Low Altitude Navigation and Targeting Infra-Red for Night (LANTIRN) pod then in use by the USAF. This proposal envisioned using only the AN/AAQ-14 targeting pod and incorporating its Litton GPS/INS. VF-103 became the first squadron to complete the Tactical Advanced Strike Syllabus and was selected to conduct the initial LANTIRN tests.

F-14B, 161608, was chosen as the test aircraft, and appropriately, "FLIRCAT" nose art was applied to the radome. *Kaminski*

Lockheed Martin LANTIRN pods significantly enhanced the Tomcat's precision strike capability. The rear cockpits of LANTIRN-equipped F-14As were modified with new, large, square Programmable Tactical Information Display. Due to the high cost involved, only seventy-five were purchased for fleet use. *Author*

During tests in 1995, 161608 delivered several GBU-16 laser-guided bombs, confirming the potential of the system. Following these successful trials, VF-103 introduced the LANTIRN to fleet service during a six-month cruise aboard the USS *Enterprise* (CVN-65), commencing June 28, 1996. All subsequent Air Wing deployments included LANTIRN-equipped Tomcats. The LANTIRN 40K was introduced in 2001 for operations above 40,000 feet. In 2003, the GBU-38 Joint Direct Attack Munition (JDAM) was added to an already impressive arsenal of laser- and GPS-guided munitions. Further upgrades involved the integration of night vision goggles with LANTIRN.

"Bombcat" F-14A, 162689, VF-41, September 1993. *Author*

"Strike Cat," F-14A, 160394, assigned to VF-41, photographed hauling a pair of CBUs over the Chocolate Mountains near El Centro in August 1994. The F-14A/B/D was cleared to deliver the entire array of cluster bombs. *Filardi*

Inert 500-pound BDU-45/B bombs fitted with BSU-86/B high-drag fins about to be loaded on F-14B, 163215, assigned to VF-103, photographed in September 1995. A month later, these tail markings would disappear, replaced with the skull and crossbones of the "Jolly Rogers." This Tomcat was the first Block 150 and was delivered December 1, 1988. *Author*

A pair of ADM-141 Tactical Air Launched Decoys mounted on triple ejector racks. TALDs present a realistic threat signature. Over thirty-nine ADM-141s were launched during Operation Deliberate Force, forcing adversaries to activate their air defense systems—which then became easy prey for HARMS. *Filardi*

The Mediterranean Sea, March 21, 2003. Aviation Ordnance personnel assigned to Fighter Squadron 32 transfer 2,000-pound GBU-31 Joint Direct Attack Munitions for uploading to an F-14B Tomcat fighter. JDAMs are guidance kits that convert existing unguided bombs into precision-guided "smart" munitions. The tail section contains an inertial navigational system (INS) and a global positioning system (GPS). A JDAM improves the accuracy of unguided bombs in any weather condition. *Osborne*

An aviation ordnanceman moves 2,000-pound bombs configured as Mk. 84 Joint Direct Attack Munitions onto an aircraft elevator aboard the USS *Kennedy* (CV-67) on March 2, 2002, during OEF. *Hampshire*

USS *Constellation* (CV-64), March 23, 2003. An F-14D Super Tomcat from Fighter Squadron 2 (VF-2) is prepared for another mission while armed with a pair GBU-16 and a pair of GBU-12 laser-guided bombs in support of Operation Iraqi Freedom. *McLain*

Onboard the US Navy (USN) aircraft carrier USS *Enterprise* (CVN-65). USN aviation personnel, assigned to VF-211, upload a GBU-16 Paveway II 1,000-pound laser-guided bomb onto a USN F-14 Tomcat while conducting flight operations in the Arabian Sea. *Reterski*

The final air-to-ground enhancement was ROVER, Remotely Operated Video Enhanced Receiver. This off-the-shelf modification cost approximately $800 per aircraft. ROVER allowed forward-deployed ground controllers to see in real time what the Tomcat aircrew was seeing. Before ROVER, ground controllers had to talk the Tomcat crew onto the target. Both VF-31 and VF-213 received these upgrades during their final Tomcat cruise, September 1, 2005, to March 10, 2006.

F-14A, 159455, assigned to NATC's Strike Test Directorate. It was photographed delivering a GBU-24 during May 1996 trials conducted near NAS Patuxent River, NATC. Of interest are the external fuel tanks modified as camera pods to record weapons separation. *US Navy*

ROVER-equipped F-14D, 164602, assigned to VF-213 and photographed November 26, 2005. The tiny blue ROVER antenna can be seen just aft of the curve of the nearest Phoenix pallet. *Timmester*

F-14A, 161292, assigned to VF-1 and photographed at NAS Fallon in June 1983. Of interest is the Heater-Ferris scheme, similar to those applied to VF-301/302 F-4S Phantoms. *Grove*

F-14A, 158627, was the first Tomcat assigned to VF-1. It was flown directly from Calverton, arriving at Miramar on June 30, 1973. "Wolfpack" originally appeared on the nose of this aircraft forward of the side number. These markings were short lived, soon being moved to the vertical stabilizer and then completely removed. *Lock*

F-14A, 162597, was delivered to VF-1 in October 1985 and photographed during October 1991. It was SARDIP/Destroyed at Grumman, St. Augustine, Florida, on February 18, 1999, following service with VF-154. *Author*

F-14D(R), 159630, VF-2, wearing the Grumman/Northrop Tomcat twenty-fifth-anniversary scheme. This honor was bestowed upon VF-2 since they had flown the Tomcat longer than any other squadron. BuNo 159630 was selected for this tribute to the Tomcat's longevity. *Twomey*

F-14A, 158629, photographed at NAS Miramar about the same time it was delivered to VF-2 via VF-124 on June 27, 1973. This Tomcat crashed on June 18, 2000, while assigned to VF-101 and performing a Tomcat flight demo at the NAS Willow Grove Air Show. Lt. William J. "Dewar" Dey and Lt. David "Fur" Bergstrom lost their lives in this crash. *Author's collection*

F-14D, 163894, assigned to the "Bounty Hunters" of VF-2 on June 2, 2003, following the squadron's final Tomcat cruise. Note the impressive scoreboard adorning the area under the canopy. *Author*

F-14D, 163900, to the "Red Rippers" of VF-11, landing at NAS Miramar on October 23, 1995. The squadron moved from Oceana to Miramar on February 26, 1992, trading in their F-14As for F-14Ds. They moved back to Oceana on November 11, 1996, transitioning to the F-14B in February 1997. *Author*

F-14A, 159025, VF-11, photographed at NAS Fallon in July 1981 during air wing workups for CVW-3's first cruise, to the Caribbean, aboard the USS *John F. Kennedy* (CV-67), between October 29, 1981, and December 11, 1981. This Tomcat is currently displayed aboard the USS *Yorktown*, Patriot's Point, South Carolina. *Grove*

Air-to-air study of "Red Ripper" F-14B(UPGRADE), 163409, photographed October 21, 2004. The squadron had recently returned from its final Tomcat cruise in support of Operation Iraqi Freedom, where they contributed 1,300 sorties and 3,100 flight hours and delivered ten GBU-16s. This Tomcat was delivered to AMARC on April 11, 2005. As we go to press, it is still listed as in storage there. *Author*

F-14A, 161855, VF-14, photographed on the NAS Oceana ramp during June 1994. It proudly displays markings commemorating the seventy-fifth anniversary of the "Tophatters," established in 1919, which are considered the oldest continuously serving squadron in the fleet. This Tomcat was remanufactured at Grumman's facility at St. Augustine, Florida, emerging as F-14B(KM-6). The KM indicates the location of the upgrade, and the -6 indicated it was the sixth F-14A upgraded to F-14B standards. *Grove*

F-14A, 159593, VF-14, NAS Miramar, on November 20, 1976. Most squadrons applied a paint scheme to commemorate the American bicentennial. This scheme was one of the best. This Tomcat was SARDIP/Destroyed at NAS Norfolk on July 1, 1993. *Logan*

F-14A, 162698, VF-14, on November 9, 2001, the day the "Tophatters" returned from their final Tomcat cruise after delivering the first strikes in the War on Terror. During their brief participation in OEF, the "Tophatters" contributed 173,324 pounds of ordnance, including 174 laser-guided bombs. *Author*

The "Freelancers" retired their last F-4 Phantom on November 4, 1983. The black-trimmed radome of F-14A, 161617, is a carryover from the squadron's Phantom scheme. The squadron represented some of the first US assets to arrive following Iraq's invasion of Kuwait. The "Freelancers" flew combat air patrols during Operation Desert Shield. *US Navy*

"OOP ACK BABY!" F-14A, 161610, with Berkeley Breathed's "Bill the Cat" from *Bloom County* adorning the vertical stabilizer, at NAF Atsugi, Japan, in July 1987. This Tomcat was stricken on March 12, 1996, during night carrier qualifications (CQ) operations, when it suffered a ramp strike causing the Tomcat to erupt in flames. The crew, Lt. Bob "Buddha" Mills and Tom "Boog" Powell, ejected successfully. *Toshiyuki*

Beautiful in-flight study of F-14A, 159617, assigned to VF-24 during May 1982. Delivered on September 18, 1975, this Tomcat was written off during an ACM engagement with a VF-126 Skyhawk on June 14, 1982. After an audible thump, the Tomcat entered a spin, first to the left, then to the right. The crew, Lt. Ed "Dragon" Riley and LCdr. George "Gatsby" Sottile, ejected successfully below 1,000 feet. *Baranek*

The "Thief of Baghdad," F-14A+, 163411, was the last of its type constructed. Photographed at NAS Fallon in November 1990, assigned to VF-24, and wearing a temporary, water-based paint scheme. This Tomcat was written off on March 15, 1993, when it suffered a catastrophic in-flight breakup. The crew, Lt. Bill "Aquaman" Daisley and LCdr. Fred "Zippo" Dillingham, perished in the crash. *Grove*

The Renegades of VF-24 operated the F-14A+ from 1989 until the conclusion of their 1991 Operation Desert Storm / Southern Watch cruise in the Persian Gulf. This example, F-14B, 163225, was photographed at NAS Miramar on August 10, 1989. It was SARDIP/ Destroyed at NAS Oceana on August 4, 2004, following service with VF-103, VF-102, and VF-101. *Anselmo*

F-14A, 159009, was the seventieth Tomcat delivered to the Navy. Photographed at NAS Oceana on November 8, 1982, this particular paint scheme became known as the "Flying Pencil" for obvious reasons. Only 3,271 flight hours were accumulated by this cat before its retirement to AMARC on July 31, 1991, where it was scrapped on January 8, 2008. *Author's collection*

F-14D, 164348, was photographed at the Roswell International Air Center during Roving Sands '97. Roving Sands was one of the largest joint air exercises in the world. *Author*

Currently displayed at NASM's Udvar-Hazy facility, F-14D(R), 159610, was photographed May 6, 2003, immediately following the Tomcatters 2002–03 Operation Enduring Freedom cruise. In a past life, as an F-14A, this Tomcat downed a Libyan MiG-23 on January 4, 1989. *Author*

F-14D, 164603, VF-31, departing NAS Fallon on May 9, 2005. The final deployment of the Tomcat to Fallon took place during May 2005. *Author*

On July 26, 1974, VF-32 flew the first Atlantic Fleet's Tomcat, 159008, to NAS Oceana. Cdr. Allen Fancher piloted the delivery flight with Lt(jg) D. C. Leestma occupying the rear seat. This view of 159008 was photographed landing aboard the USS *John F. Kennedy* (CVA-67). The large yellow number "1" painted on the fuselage indicates that the squadron was the recipient of the Admiral Joseph Clifton Award as the Navy's top fighter squadron. VF-32 was the first Tomcat squadron to receive this award. *Author's collection*

F-14A, 159444, at NAS Oceana on April 30, 1983. Delivered on December 6, 1974, it would serve for almost twenty years. On March 31, 1992, it was placed in storage at AMARC and was subsequently scrapped on May 14, 2007. *Paul*

F-14B (UPGRADE), 162916, assigned to VF-32 on January 13, 2004. Note the full load of six Phoenix. This event marked the first time an operational squadron would launch six AIM-54s on one sortie. Five successfully launched, but the sixth fell free, the rocket motor failing to ignite. This Tomcat is currently displayed in this scheme at the Richard J. Gross VFW post, East Berlin, Pennsylvania. *Author*

During the waning Tomcat days, F-14 squadrons were permitted to paint one jet in a retro scheme. Photographed on August 25, 2005, this F-14B(UPGRADE), 162691, wears a 1970s retro scheme. Delivered to AMARC on September 28, 2005, it still resides there as we go to press. *Author*

Unofficially known as "the Batmobile," F-14A, 159428, is shown here on May 6, 1982. On June 17, 1984, it suffered Class B damage during a ramp strike aboard the USS *America* (CV-66). *McGarry*

On April 17, 1991, CVW-1 returned to NAS Oceana following Operation Desert Storm. Combat missions consisted of TARPS Escort, high-value unit (HVU) CAP, DEFCAP, and MiG Sweeps. The VF-33 Tomcat pictured is F-14A, 160390. It downed an Su-22 during the first Gulf of Sidra Incident, August 19, 1981. This Tomcat was written off October 25, 1994, when it crashed into the sea while landing aboard the USS *Abraham Lincoln*. The first female Tomcat pilot, Lt. Kara "Hulk" Hultgreen, perished in the accident. *Author*

F-14A, 160388, photographed on the deck of the USS *Nimitz* (CVN-68) during the 1978 Mediterranean Sea cruise. This Tomcat was delivered on March 24, 1977. It accumulated only 978 flight hours, 333 catapult launches, and 343 arrested landings, including field arrestments, before crashing on April 1, 1980, on approach to the USS *Nimitz*. *Romano*

F-14A, 162608, a.k.a. "Anna," shortly after returning from Operation Enduring Freedom on November 9, 2001. During their last Tomcat cruise, the squadron dropped 200,000 pounds of laser-guided ordnance on Taliban and al-Qaeda targets. This Tomcat resides at the Southern Museum of Flight, Birmingham, Alabama. *Author*

F-14A, 160661, assigned to VF-51 and photographed rolling in on a formation of Grumman A-6 Intruders in June 1983. The "Screaming Eagles" were the first Tomcat squadron to intercept a Russian Tu-22 Backfire bomber by using the television camera sight (TCS). The squadron also participated in the filming of the movie *Top Gun*. Foster

A "Screaming Eagles" F-14A, 160686, during air wing workups at NAS Fallon before the 1992 Operation Southern Watch cruise in the Persian Gulf. The squadron's final cruise, WestPac / Indian Ocean, took place aboard the USS *Kitty Hawk* (CV-63) between June 24, 1994, and December 22, 1994. *Grove*

F-14A, 162707, was involved in a somewhat unusual aerial victory. On September 22, 1987, while taking part in exercise display determination, it downed USAF RF-4C, 69-0381, with a Sidewinder. The crew of the Phantom survived. *US Navy*

F-14A+, 161870, photographed March 27, 1991, returning from Operation Desert Storm. The "Be-devilers" were the first fleet squadron to receive the F-14A+, on August 11, 1988. This Tomcat was delivered to AMARC on December 9, 2004, and was scrapped on June 18, 2008. *Author*

F-14B, 161432, May 26, 1994. Although still displaying VF-74 markings, 161432 was assigned to VF-101 when photographed on May 26, 1994. The squadron spent its final days providing adversary aircraft to the fleet; hence the nonstandard paint scheme. This Tomcat was later assigned to VX-9 at Point Mugu. It was SARDIP/Destroyed at NADEP Jacksonville on March 29, 2004. *Kaston*

Not yet possessing a Tomcat of their own, VF-84 borrowed 159013 from VF-32 and painted it as their own, complete with the "Jolly Roger," for this official squadron PR shot. *VF-84 via Barto*

During Operation Desert Storm, CVW-8 squadrons were permitted to apply nose art to one aircraft. F-14A, 162692, became "Cat Snatch Fever." Unfortunately, she was sanitized before her June 26, 1991, homecoming. *Morgan*

Photographed during the filming of the sci-fi cult classic *The Final Countdown*, this "Jolly Rogers" Tomcat displays kill markings signifying the shoot-down of a pair of Japanese Zeros. *Force*

The VF-84 "Jolly Rogers"' swan song was the filming of *Executive Decision* (1995). Note the attention to detail, including live air-to-air ordnance, or at least painted to represent live ordnance. The squadron disestablished on October 1, 1995, but their history and the "Bones" passed onto VF-103. *Skarbek*

F-14A, 160402, VF-101, October 1978. This Tomcat was one of three damaged or destroyed aboard the USS *Nimitz* on May 26, 1981, when struck by an EA-6B. Rebuilt, it returned to service with VF-101. It was delivered to AMARC on January 10, 1996, and was scrapped on May 5, 2007. *Paul*

F-14A+, 162915, being delivered to VF-101 on April 1, 1988. The new variant cured the F-14's most severe problem, that of sensitive and troublesome engines: the previous TF-30s were replaced by GE F110s, providing a 14,600-pound increase in thrust over the F-14A. Following service with VF-32, this Tomcat was SARDIP/Destroyed at NAS Oceana on September 29, 2005. *Author*

Final demo, baby! A Tomcat Flight Demo was always the highlight of any Naval Air Station air show. Enthusiasts traveled from around the world to attend the last official Tomcat flight demo on Sunday, September 18, 2005, at NAS Oceana. The following day, this F-14D, 164601, was flown west to the Castle AFB air museum, where it resides today. *Author*

April 17, 1991, "Diamondbacks," 162704, returning from Operation Desert Storm. During ODS, VF-102 Tomcats flew MiG Sweep, HVUCAP, TARPS, SCUDCAP, and BARCAP missions. This Tomcat was SARDIP/ Destroyed at NAS Oceana on April 15, 1999. *Author*

F-14A, 161155, assigned to VF-102, photographed aboard the USS *America* during the "Diamondbacks" Mediterranean cruise, December 2, 1991, to June 6, 1992, in support of Operation Southern Watch. *Romano*

F-14B, 163225, photographed on March 27, 2002, the day after the squadron's homecoming from OEF. During this deployment, VF-102 flew 5,000 combat hours and dropped 50,000 pounds of precision ordnance. BuNo 163225 transferred to VF-101 the day after the homecoming. It was SARDIP/Destroyed on August 4, 2004. *Author*

Yellow flight helmets were a "Slugger" trademark. This VF-103, F-14A, 160893, was photographed during a May 1987 training flight. *Baranek*

F-14B, 163219, on the NAS Fallon ramp in October 1991. On March 17, 2000, it was written off following a crash 250 miles southwest of Bermuda. The crew, Lt. Scott Guimond and LCdr. Thomas Eberhard, ejected, suffering minor injuries. *Grove*

Delivered as an F-14A on June 1, 1984, 161855 was upgraded to F-14B standards at Grumman's St. Augustine facility during 1994. Photographed in flight with a Legacy Hornet in April 2002, it was SARDIP/Destroyed at NAS Jacksonville on March 31, 2004, following service with VF-101. *Author*

F-14B, 162924, on Alert 5 status aboard the USS *Enterprise*, May 1996. This cruise was VF-103's first as "Jolly Rogers." It was also the first for the LANTIRN targeting system. *Author*

F-14B, 163217, taxis in for the final Tomcat homecoming of the "Jolly Rogers" on December 13, 2004. The squadron's first F/A-18F was present to welcome the unit home from Operation Iraqi Freedom. This Tomcat was delivered to AMARC on January 26, 2005, and was scrapped on March 12, 2008. *Author*

VF-103 SLUGGERS/JOLLY ROGERS

TOMCAT SQUADRONS 57

F-14A, 160674, photographed at NAS Fallon in June 1980. It was written off a year later, on June 27, 1981, when it crashed into the Indian Ocean. The crew, LCdr. D. McCort, and Lt. D. Pittman, successfully ejected. *Grove*

F-14A, 161621; Lt. Mike Conn, a Tomcat RIO assigned to VF-111, painted "Miss Molly." The nose art was a tribute to Ms. Molly Snead, a nurse who provided care to Congressman Carl Vinson's wife. Initially, a COD servicing the USS *Carl Vinson* was named Miss Molly. When it was learned Ms. Snead had become seriously ill, the request was made to paint Sundowner 200 as "Miss Molly." *Gupta*

F-14A, 162594, a.k.a. the "Buick" or "Jeepney," was photographed at NAF Andrews on November 1990. This cat was stricken on October 3, 2002, while assigned to VF-101. It crashed into the Gulf of Mexico while on a training flight. It made news on May 6, 2006, when a vertical stabilizer from this Tomcat washed ashore on a beach near West Cork, Ireland. *Author*

A beautiful takeoff shot of F-14A 159852, July 1978. The Aardvark dates to the squadron's F-4 Phantom II days, borrowed with permission from cartoonist Johnny Hart's "BC" comic strip. *Picciani*

F-14A, 159874, was the fiftieth and final Block 90 Tomcat constructed. It was delivered on December 1, 1976, and administratively stricken at NAS Norfolk on February 1, 1995. It was photographed at NAS Fallon during predeployment training in September 1983. Of interest are the orange flight suits, a hallmark of VF-114 aircrew. *Grove*

F-14A, 159637, was the last 'Vark assigned to VF-114. It made the squadron's final flight on November 30, 1992. The "Aardvarks" disestablished on April 30, 1993. *Puzzullo*

F-14A, 158636, photographed August 1974, nearly a year after delivery to VF-124. On November 5, 1975, it was transferred to the Atlantic Fleet FRS, VF-101. It was SARDIP/Destroyed at NAS Norfolk following an accident aboard the USS *Enterprise* on September 23, 2003, while assigned to VF-211. *Van Geffen*

"Gunslinger 76," F-14A, 159616, displayed one of the best US bicentennial schemes of any squadron during 1976. This Tomcat was delivered on September 9, 1975, and retired at NAS Patuxent River on September 1, 1994. Its last assignment involved use as a trainer. *Grove*

F-14A, 161165, being spotted on the deck of the USS *Ranger* on March 4, 1982. CQ or carrier qualifications is still the most challenging part of becoming a naval aviator. *Svendsen*

The "Gunfighters" first F-14D Super Tomcat arrived on November 16, 1990. This example, 163903, was delivered on May 31, 1991. Following VF-124's disestablishment on September 30, 1994, all Tomcat training was transferred to VF-101. The "Grim Reapers" maintained an F-14D training detachment at Miramar until September 1996. *Author*

A beautiful action shot of F-14A, 159431, taken during October 1975. VF-142 transitioned to the Tomcat at NAS Miramar and then moved to NAS Oceana during April 1975. *Leader*

The rattlesnake applied to the side of 159453, in a photo dated May 11, 1978, indicates this Tomcat was assigned to legendary naval aviator Alex "Rattler" Rucker. This pit viper also adorned Tomcats assigned to VF-14 and VF-101. *Paul*

Deck crew aboard the USS *Dwight D. Eisenhower* (CVN-69) examine damage to F-14B, 161433. The crew made an emergency landing on November 13, 1991, after its radome separated in flight, shattering the windscreen and canopy. Despite his injuries, the pilot, LCdr. Joe Edwards, landed safely aboard the "*Ike.*" Both he and his RIO, LCdr. Scott Grundmeier, received the Distinguished Flying Cross. LCdr. Edwards later became a space shuttle pilot. F-14B, 161433, was returned to service. It was SARDIP/Destroyed at NAS Oceana on March 10, 2005. *Catt*

F-14B, 162926, departing Oceana on March 15, 2005. It was painted in a "Pukin' Dogs" retro scheme for this flight and for induction in the New England Air Museum, Windsor Locks, Connecticut. *Author*

Tomcats not flown to AMARC or air museums became scrap. On April 6, 2005, the remains of VF-143 F-14B, 162924, were photographed being towed to Oceana's boneyard to be cut up. *Author*

The crew responsible for the beautiful retro paint scheme applied to F-14B 162926, poses for one final photo with their Tomcat prior to its departure for the New England Air Museum. *Author*

F-14A, 159457, photographed during January 1977. The tail markings leave no doubt this Tomcat is assigned to the "Pukin' Dogs." *Lock*

F-14B, 162921, photographed on April 6, 1998, participating in Operation Southern Watch. This Tomcat was delivered to AMARC on December 22, 2004, and was scrapped on June 18, 2008. *Davis*

F-14B, 163220, photographed at NAS Oceana on September 18, 2002, weeks after returning from Operation Enduring Freedom. *Author*

F-14A, 161141, "Miss Shelly," on April 11, 1998. This Tomcat is currently on museum display at NAF Atsugi, Japan. *Davis*

On September 24, 2003, F-14, 161866, departs NAF Atsugi, Japan, for the last time. It arrived at its destination, AMARC, on October 23, 2003, following a stop at NAS Oceana. *Call*

F-14A, 161298, was photographed at the MCAS Beaufort Air Show on April 1988. Following the squadron's disestablishment, it was assigned to VF-114 and written off on May 17, 1990, when it crashed in restricted area 2301 during an ACM engagement. *Kopack*

F-14A, 161626, photographed near NAS Miramar, California. This Tomcat was delivered to AMARC by VF-41 on January 25, 2002. It was returned to service with VF-101 on January 18, 2003. It was returned to AMARC by VF-211 on September 13, 2004, and was scrapped on July 22, 2009. *LeGare*

F-14A, 158637, was the last Block 65 Tomcat constructed. It was rebuilt to Block 135 standards, including TARPS capability. Following the disestablishment of VF-201, this Tomcat was transferred to VF-211. Damaged aboard the USS *Enterprise* on September 23, 2003, it was SARDIPed at NAS Norfolk and officially stricken on January 6, 2004. *Jordan*

The Superheats received 162710 on March 25, 1987. It was photographed at NAF Andrews during March 1994. Following the disestablishment of VF-202, it was transferred to VF-101. On September 5, 1997, 162710 was delivered to the National Naval Aviation Museum, NAS Pensacola, Florida. *Author*

F-14A, 159626, photographed at NAS Miramar during February 1976, before the squadron received its full complement of Tomcats. Note the bright-red covers over the engine inlets, designed to prevent foreign-object damage (FOD) when conducting engine run-ups. *Lock*

F-14BA+, 161599, VF-211, photographed at Bergstrom AFB, participating in RAM '90, the international, biennial photo reconnaissance meet. *Author*

F-14A 158618 assigned to VF-211, taxiing at NAS Oceana during work-ups for CVW-9's November 2001 – May 2002, WestPac, Northern Arabian Sea cruise. This Tomcat was written off when the tailhook separated while attempting to land aboard the USS *John C. Stennis* (CVN-74), March 8, 2002. The crew ejected and were rescued. *Author*

Beautiful in-flight study of 161271 during May 1998. This F-14A is equipped with TARPS; hence, no
LANTIRN pod is mounted. *Baranek*

F-14A, 161612, VF-211, photographed on September 12, 2004, departing NAS Oceana and heading for retirement at AMARC, Davis-Monthan AFB, Arizona. This Tomcat was scrapped on July 22, 2009. *Author*

F-14A, 159857, hoisted aboard the USS *Kitty Hawk* (CV-63) on October 20, 1977, for the VF-213's inaugural Tomcat cruise. *Lock*

A month after returning from OEF on January 23, 2002, F-14D, 164344, displays an impressive scoreboard of combat missions. Also, the Blacklions earned the Battle "E," Safety "S," CNO Clifton, and CFWL Golden Wrench awards for 2001. *Author*

Displaying a retro paint scheme, Blacklions, F-14D, 164602, parked on the NAS Fallon ramp on May 9, 2005. This deployment was the last one for the Tomcat at NAS Fallon. *Author*

F-14A, 158630, hauling inert ordnance in the form of 4X Iron Bombs, 2X AIM54s, and 2X AIM-9s. VF-301 built an outstanding safety record of more than 71,000 hours without a Class A mishap. *Jordan*

F-14A, 158980, NAS Miramar, in June 1990 (top). This Tomcat spent its entire service career at NAS Miramar, accumulating only 2,287 flight hours, 312 catapult launches, and 314 arrested landings, including field arrestments. It was retired to AMARC on September 13, 1990 (below). *Knowles/Van Winkle*

F-14A, 159830, photographed at NAS Miramar in February 1978, displaying the Ferris "Splinter" scheme named after its originator, artist Keith Ferris. This Tomcat was painted in a nonstandard scheme for AIMVAL/ACEVAL. Conducted over the Nevada desert during 1976–77, these evaluations verified aerial-combat principles dating back to World War II. *Grove*

Shortly after the 1991 Tailhook scandal, the Bunny was sanitized and removed from F-14A 159853. On May 22, 1992, the day this Tomcat was scheduled to depart for the Navy's rework facility, VX-4's illustrator used his original Bunny stencil, applying it to a piece of white cardstock, and added a teardrop. The temporary marking was taped to the vertical stabilizer. Interested VX-4 personnel used it as a backdrop for photographs, and quite a few did, but mostly they were maintenance crews, not officers, due to the fact these markings were not officially approved/sanctioned. *Roth*

F-14A, 159853, the "Black Bunny," assigned to VX-4. The famous Playboy Bunny motif was changed to the more acceptable Bat design when the squadron merged with VX-5 to become VX-9. *Roth*

F-14D, 164599, assigned to VX-9 on October 17, 2003. VX-4 disestablished on September 30, 1994, and its assets were allocated to VX-9. This Tomcat was delivered to AMARC on June 23, 2004, and was scrapped on July 21, 2009. *Kaston*

NF-14D, 163415, assigned to VX-30, was used for F-14D development flight test work until its retirement to AMARC on June 29, 2004. It was scrapped there on July 21, 2009. The "N" prefix signified that the airframe was modified for test purposes. *Kaminski*

F-14A, 158625, PMTC, on June 8, 1992, showing a left underside view of an F-14 Tomcat aircraft before the launch of an advanced, medium-range, air-to-air missile (AMRAAM) at the Pacific Missile Test Center. *Thornsley*

NF-14B, 163223, NAWC Weapons Division, on December 14, 1995. This Tomcat was delivered to AMARC on June 17, 2004, and was scrapped on June 17, 2008. *Vasquez*

F-14A, 158614, on the ramp of an unidentified USAF base, December 29, 1972. The stylized "W" on the vertical stabilizer indicates that this Tomcat was assigned to NATC's Weapons Test Division. What appears to be a TCS chin pod is the AN/ALR-23 IRST pod. *Author's collection*

F-14A, 158620, assigned to Strike Test Directorate and photographed on the NATC ramp in October 1986. This was one of twenty-six rebuilt to Block 135 standards and delivered to Reserve Squadron (RS) VF-201. It was written off during OEF while assigned to VF-154. The crew ejected due to a fuel transfer issue and were rescued by the crew of a USAF HH-60G assigned to the 301st RS. *Author*

F-14A, 161623, is one of lowest-time Tomcats surviving. It was delivered on February 29, 1984, and accumulated 789 flight hours, zero catapult launches, and zero traps. Grumman modified this Tomcat with a full F-14D avionics suite while retaining the TF30-PW-414A power plants. It was retired October 1, 1993, and is on display at NATC Patuxent River, Maryland. *Graser*

NF-14D, 163412, NAWC Aircraft Division; flew for the first time on July 14, 1995, using DFCS designed to help protect aircrew from unrecoverable flat spins and carrier landing mishaps. Following service with VX-9, it was delivered to AMARC on April 9, 2002, and was scrapped on July 21, 2009. *Kaminski*

F-14A, 159855, displays a paint scheme similar to one worn by the Soviet Su-27 Flanker. This Tomcat was photographed in April 1996, months before NFWS (a.k.a. TOPGUN) became part of Naval Strike Warfare Center and Carrier Airborne Early Warning Weapons School (TOPDOME) and Strike University (STRIKE U), to form Naval Strike and Air Warfare Center (NSAWC) at NAS Fallon, Nevada. The last Tomcats departed NSAWC in early October 2003. *Roth*

F-14A 162591, assigned to NSAWC and photographed at NAS Oceana, November 9, 2001. On January 31, 2002, this Tomcat was retired to the Quonset Air Museum, Quonset Point, Rhode Island. When that museum closed, the Tomcat was transferred to the United States Naval Academy at Annapolis, Maryland, where it is displayed today.

F-14A, 161137, photographed on the NADC ramp in May 1990. The Tomcat pilot on staff at this time was future Navy captain and NASA astronaut Winston Elliott Scott. VF-101 retired this Tomcat to AMARC on May 21, 1996, and it was scrapped there on June 18, 2008. TARPS was one of the significant contributions made to the Tomcat's mission by the Naval Air Development Center, Warminster, Pennsylvania. *Author*

Grumman Tomcats were utilized to support two major projects conducted by NASA/Dryden. F-14A, 157991 (1X), was used in high-angle-of-attack and spin recovery tests. NASA 991 was configured for single-pilot flight. A spin recovery parachute was installed between the vertical stabilizers on the beavertail. The program included 212 test flights and was successful in improving the Tomcats' AOA flying qualities. Lessons learned were incorporated into the F-14D, Super Tomcat. F-14A, 158613, was assigned No. 834 and utilized by NASA to test laminar-flow studies during the Variable Sweep Transition Flight Experimental (VSTFE) Program from 1986 to 1987. The Tomcat was an obvious choice for these tests because of the variable sweep, high Mach, and wing pressure distribution. The program investigated laminar-to-turbulent transition location for transport aircraft then under design. *NASA*

CHAPTER 8
The Tomcat Bares Its Claws

F-14A, 159000, assigned to VF-1, photographed on September 28, 1974, during the Tomcat's first cruise to the waters off the coast of South Vietnam. *Curtis*

Although deployed to the waters off the coast of Vietnam from September 17, 1974, to May 20, 1975, the Tomcats of VF-1 and VF-2 did not engage in combat. Instead, they flew reconnaissance missions and provided combat air patrol (CAP) during Operation Frequent Wind, the evacuation of Americans from Saigon.

One year later, 1976, Tomcats were once again called upon to cover the withdrawal of US citizens, this time from Beirut, Lebanon, during Operation Fluid Drive. During Operation Eagle Claw, in April 1980, F-14A squadrons were deployed to the region, tasked with providing cover for US forces attempting to rescue hostages held by Iran. The mission failed. Eight US servicemen and one Iranian civilian lost their lives as a result.

F-14A, 158997, assigned to the "Bounty Hunters" of VF-2, preparing for launch from the USS *Enterprise* (CVN-65) during Operation Frequent Wind. *US Navy*

F-14A Tomcats assigned to VF-41 and VF-84 aboard the USS *Nimitz* (CVN-68) during April 1980. The recognition stripes on the wings indicate that these squadrons were participating in Operation Eagle Claw. These markings were used to distinguish US aircraft from similar types flown by the Iranians. The VF-41 Tomcat closest to the camera is 160385. *US Navy*

F-14A 160398 assigned to the "Black Aces" of VF-41 and photographed during August 1982 aboard the USS *Nimitz* (CVN-68). The yellow "1" on the vertical stabilizer indicates VF-41 was awarded the coveted Admiral Clifton Award, recognizing meritorious achievement by a fighter squadron. The Safety "S" and Battle "E" also indicate the squadron was awarded the CNO's Aviation Safety Award and the Battle Effectiveness Award. *Author*

F-14A 160406 assigned to the "Jolly Rogers" of VF-84 preparing to launch from the USS *Nimitz* (CVN-68), August 1982. Deck crew surrounding this Tomcat wear different color jerseys to identify their various responsibilities. For example, the green jersey at the nose wheel is part of the catapult and arresting gear crew. The yellow jersey near the nose of the aircraft is a plane director or aircraft handling officer. The red jersey could be a member of the crash crew, ordnancemen, or EOD. *Author*

F-14A, 160390, Fast Eagle 107, on the NAS Oceana ramp on February 12, 1982. This Su-22 killer was written off on October 25, 1994, when it departed controlled flight on approach to the USS *Abraham Lincoln*, resulting in the death of Lt. Kara Hultgreen, the Navy's first carrier-based female fighter pilot. *Jay*

On August 19, 1981, F-14A Tomcats shot down two Libyan air force Su-22s. This engagement took place in a region of the Mediterranean known as the Gulf of Sidra. The USS *Nimitz* (CVN-68) was participating in a Freedom of Navigation exercise in the Gulf. A pair of F-14As assigned to VF-41 (160390 and 160403) were engaged and fired upon by two Libyan Su-22 Fitters. The F-14As responded with AIM-9L Sidewinders, destroying both Libyan aircraft.

Commencing October 25, 1983, F-14s assigned to VF-14 and VF-32, flying from the deck of the USS *Independence* (CV-62), flew CAP and reconnaissance missions, with TARPS, in support of Operation Urgent Fury, the invasion of Grenada.

Tensions in the Middle East remained high throughout the 1980s, and Tomcats were once again flying CAP and reconnaissance missions, this time over Lebanon. On December 3, 1983, a pair of F-14As assigned to VF-31 were fired upon by Syrian surface-to-air missile sites and antiaircraft artillery based in the Bekaa Valley. The Tomcats recovered aboard the USS *John F. Kennedy* (CV-67), having suffered no damage. The following day a retaliatory air strike was conducted on these positions, with CAP provided by Tomcats.

On October 10, 1985, F-14As from VF-74 and VF-103 launched from the deck of the USS *Saratoga* (CV-60). Their mission was to intercept an Egypt Air Boeing 737 carrying the hijackers who had taken over the cruise ship MS *Achille Lauro*. This hijacking resulted in the death of American Leon Klinghoffer. Intelligence

F-14A, 160403, NAS Oceana, on February 12, 1982. On August 19, 1981, this Tomcat and Fast Eagle 107, 160390, downed a pair of Libyan Su-22 Fitters. Note the kill marking on the vertical stabilizer. *Jay*

A "Sluggers" F-14A, 161156, photographed aboard the USS *Saratoga* (CV-60) in early 1986. *Shayka*

F-14A, 160906, assigned to VF-74 and photographed at NAS Oceana on April 20, 1985, after completing their Fleet Fighter ACM Readiness Program (FFARP), an intensive three-week ACM training program requiring as many as thirty sorties a day flown on the instrumented TACTS Range. *Paul*

sources discovered that the terrorists were attempting to escape Egypt, seeking refuge in Tunisia. With the aid of an EA-6B Prowler and E-2C Hawkeye, the Egypt Air 737 was successfully intercepted and diverted to Naval Air Station Sigonella, Sicily, and the hijackers were taken into custody.

On March 24, 1986, Tomcats assigned to VF-102 were fired upon by Libyan SA-5 surface-to-air missiles while taking part in Freedom of Navigation exercises in the Gulf of Sidra. This incident, the bombing of the "La Belle Discothèque" in West Berlin, plus other events led directly to Operation El Dorado Canyon, US air strikes on Libya that included CAPs provided by Tomcats from VF-33 and VF-102.

Operation Earnest Will, better known as the "Tanker War," took place between July 1987 and September 1988. While performing CAP, a pair of F-14As assigned to VF-21 launched three AIM-7 Sparrow missiles against a pair of Iranian F-4 Phantoms displaying hostile intent toward a US Navy P-3 Orion. Although an explosion was witnessed, the shoot-down of either Iranian F-4 Phantom was not confirmed.

F-14A, 159458, assigned to VF-102. The "Diamondbacks" provided combat air patrol covering an attack force consisting of F-111Fs, A-6Es, A-7Es, and F/A-18s during Operation El Dorado Canyon. *Arnold*

F-14A, 161151, armed with live AIM-7 Sparrows, photographed during VF-33's participation in Operation El Dorado Canyon. *Sagnor*

MiG-23 killer F-14A, 159437, returning to NAS Oceana on January 29, 1989. Of interest is the kill marking was sanitized from the airframe. *Author*

F-14A, 161607, is believed to be one of the two VF-21 Tomcats involved in the aforementioned Iranian incident. *Kopack*

F-14A, 159610, touching down on runway 23L, NAS Oceana, on January 29, 1989. Note the absence of the kill marking. This Tomcat was remanufactured as an F-14D(R) and is displayed at the Udvar-Hazy Annex, National Air and Space Museum. *Author*

F-14A, 162606, VF-2, photographed during May 1991, post–Operation Desert Storm. During the conflict, the "Bounty Hunters" flew 124 strike escort, 359 combat air patrol, and seventy-one photo reconnaissance missions. A total of 68.8 percent of these missions were flown at night. Besides achieving a 100 percent sortie completion rate, the squadron also set a monthly F-14 flight hour record of 1,176.5 hours. *Anselmo*

Tomcat aerial victories were nonexistent during Operation Desert Storm. One notable exception was VF-1 F-14A, 162603, crewed by Lt. Stuart "Meat" Broce and Cdr. Ron "Bongo" McElraft. On February 6, 1991, they were vectored to a bandit by a USAF E-3 Sentry. The target, an Iraqi Mi-8 helicopter, was destroyed via AIM-9 Sidewinder. This Tomcat was written off when its flight controls froze during launch from the USS *John C. Stennis* (CVN-74) on June 23, 2000. *Kaston*

On January 4, 1989, another aerial engagement took place between Libyan air force jets and US Navy aircraft. This time the players involved were a pair of MiG-23 Floggers and a pair of F-14As (159437 and 159610) assigned to VF-32 and flying from the deck of the USS *John F. Kennedy* (CV-67). This engagement lasted a total of nine minutes and resulted in both Libyan fighters

being destroyed, one via AIM-9 Sidewinder and the other via AIM-7 Sparrow.

When Iraq invaded Kuwait, two carrier battle groups built around the USS *Dwight D. Eisenhower* (CVN-69) and the USS *Independence* (CV-62) were the first US assets available to prevent a further push by Iraq into Saudi Arabia. The two carriers were equipped with four Tomcat squadrons: VF-143, VF-142, VF-154, and VF-21. The carriers and air wings were rotated during Operation Desert Shield and relieved by ten Tomcat squadrons consisting of VF-1 and VF-2, USS *Ranger* (CV-61); VF-14 and VF-32, USS *John F. Kennedy* (CV-67); VF-41 and VF-84, USS *Theodore Roosevelt* (CVN-71); VF-33 and VF-102, USS *America* (CV-66); and VF-74 and VF-103, USS *Saratoga* (CV-60). During Operation Desert Storm, F-14A/A+ Tomcats flew more than 1,400 sorties involving tactical reconnaissance with TARPS, fleet defense, protection of strike packages, and combat air patrol. Regarding the latter, the Tomcat did not enjoy the same success as its USAF counterpart, the F-15C Eagle; F-14A, 162603, scored the only Tomcat aerial victory. On February 6, 1991, assigned to VF-1, it downed an Iraqi Mi-8 helicopter with an AIM-9. One Tomcat, F-14A+ 161430, was brought down by a modified SA-2 surface-to-air missile on January 21, 1991. The pilot, Lt.Devon Jones, was rescued but his RIO, Lt. Lawrence R. Slade, was captured and held as a POW until the end of the war.

The "Tophatters" flew CAP missions starting on January 17, 1991, day one of Operation Desert Storm. This example, F-14A, 162700, photographed on March 27, 1991, displays an unusual tactical paint scheme consisting of a mix of blue and gray. *Author*

The VF-32 show cat, F-14A, 162701, was photographed on the NAS Oceana following the "Swordsmen" Operation Desert Storm homecoming on March 27, 1991. The "Swordsmen" was the first squadron to develop and employ tactics to defend strike aircraft during supersonic low-altitude missile (SLAM) deliveries. The squadron also designed survivable night surface-to-air-missile (SAM) defensive tactics for the F-14A, featuring innovative lighting configurations and sophisticated high-value unit (HVU) package maneuvering/communication procedures. *Author*

F-14A, 160399, photographed during VF-33's Operation Desert Storm (ODS) homecoming on April 17, 1991. A typical ODS mission was noted in the squadron's command history for January 28, 1991: "Skipper Snodgrass and his RIO, LCdr. Floyd, led a daytime MiG Sweep across western Iraq. Lt. Matt Bannon and LCdr. Tom Lang were assigned as HVUCAP for this mission. They were in support of a strike on scud missile sites and a suspected chemical site in the vicinity of Qasr Amij airfield in western Iraq. They targeted a flight of Iraqi MiGs approaching at high speed. As soon as the Iraqis realized they were being targeted, the Iraqi flight withdrew and did not engage. Both sweepers and HUVCAP encountered extremely heavy AAA from multiple sites. Cdr. Snodgrass and LCDR Floyd were awarded individual Air Medals with Combat 'V.' Lt. Bannon and LCdr. Lang were awarded the Navy Commendation Medal with Combat 'V.'" *Author*

F-14A, 162695, VF-102, Operation Desert Storm homecoming on April 17, 1991. During ODS, the "Diamondbacks" flew Migsweep, HUVCAP, SCUDCAP, BARCAP, and TARPS missions. This Tomcat was upgraded to F-14B and later to F-14B(UPGRADE) standards. It was delivered to AMARC on January 12, 2005, and was scrapped there on March 12, 2008. *Author*

F-14A, 162689, VF-41, aboard the USS *Theodore Roosevelt* (CVN-71) on February 7, 1991. The "Black Aces" began flying combat sorties on January 19, 1991. Missions included strike support, CAP, and TARPS CAP. The squadron remained on station following the ceasefire on March 12, 1991. The provocative nose art was sanitized before VF-41's homecoming on June 26, 1991. *Morgan*

F-14A, 162692, and also 162688 started the Desert Storm cruise in gloss gray with black tails. While en route to the war zone, both were repainted in one-tone dull gray. BuNo 162692 was repainted gloss gray with black tails before the squadron's homecoming on June 26, 1991. *Author*

Clubleaf 212, F-14A+, 161430, photographed on the ramp of NAS Oceana, Virginia. It was shot down by an Iraqi SA-2 on January 21, 1991. The pilot, Lt. Devon Jones, was rescued by a USAF MH-53 supported by A-10 Warthogs. The RIO, Lt. Lawrence R. Slade, became a POW and was released following the conflict. *Author*

F-14A+, 162919, photographed returning from Operation Desert Storm on March 27, 1991. This Tomcat was delivered to VF-74 on August 11, 1988. On April 11, 1994, it was transferred to the Aircraft Division of NAWC for ALR-67, ALQ-126B, and ALQ-167 integration tests. It was further modified to F-14B(UPGRADE) standards and assigned to VF-102 and then VF-11. On April 13, 2005, it was delivered to AMARC and was scrapped there on March 12, 2008. *Author*

F-14B, 163227, assigned to VF-102 "Diamondbacks," prepares to enter the pattern for the USS *John F. Kennedy* (CV-67). It was supporting Operation Southern Watch. *US Navy*

Following Operation Desert Storm, from February 28, 1991, until the start of Operation Enduring Freedom on October 7, 2001, several smaller yet significant operations took place involving the participation of Tomcat squadrons. Operation Provide Comfort (March 1991–January 1997), Operation Southern Watch (August 1992–March 2003), and Operation Northern Watch (January 1997–March 2003) utilized Tomcats to patrol the no-fly zones put in place following Desert Storm. F-14 sorties included CAP, TARPS, and air interdiction.

In the Balkans, Tomcats assigned to VF-41 took part in Operation Deliberate Force from August 30 to September 20, 1995. On September 5, 1995, the first laser-guided bomb was dropped from a Tomcat during combat operations. A pair of VF-41 F-14s were tasked with attacking an ammunition dump in eastern Bosnia. Because the F-14A had yet to be cleared to carry the LANTIRN pod, the target was "buddy" lased by an F/A-18C Hornet. The occasion also signified the first delivery of air-to-ground munitions by a Tomcat engaged in combat operations.

On December 16, 1998, F-14Bs assigned to VF-32 took part in the opening phase of Operation Desert Fox. The four-day bombing campaign was an attempt to force Iraq's compliance with UN resolutions. The combat debut of the F-14D Super Tomcat was made on December 19, 1998, when VF-213 joined the strike packages. Tomcats of VF-32 alone delivered over 111,000 pounds of munitions, including sixteen GBU-16, sixteen GBU-10, and twenty-six GBU-24 laser-guided bombs.

In addition to supporting Operation Southern Watch, the Tomcats of VF-41 returned to flying combat missions over the Balkans from April 9 through June 9, 1999. This time, they were joined by VF-14 for Operation Allied Force. Flying from the deck of the USS *Theodore Roosevelt* (CVN-71), both squadrons participated in airstrikes as well as conducting TARPS reconnaissance and Forward Air Control sorties. This entire campaign was fought from the air, with the last bombs of this conflict delivered by a VF-41 Tomcat.

On September 11, 2001, New York's Twin Towers were brought down by a terror attack. The USS *Enterprise* (CVN-65) was steaming for home, having completed its final Operation Southern Watch mission on September 9. The *Enterprise* Battle Group soon made a 180-degree turn, heading back to the North Arabian Sea. They were joined by USS *Carl Vinson* (CVN-70) with VF-213's F-14Ds aboard. On October 7, 2001, four VF-213 Tomcats led the first Navy air strikes of Operation Enduring Freedom (OEF). Armed with GBU-16 or GBU-12 laser-guided bombs plus one AIM-54C Phoenix, two AIM-7M Sparrows, and two AIM-9L Sidewinders, these F-14Ds launched ordnance totaling a whopping 72,000

F-14A, 161607, VF-41, in May 1996. Of interest is the single laser-guided bomb (LGB) silhouette on the nose gear door. "Black Ace" Bombcats delivered 24,000 pounds of ordnance on Bosnian Serb targets before the cessation of hostilities between August 30 and September 1, 1995. *Author*

During Operation Desert Fox, Tomcat firsts included the first GBU-24s dropped by the USN in combat, the first multiple GBU-24 deliveries by any platform in combat, the first combat use of LANTIRN, the first autonomous F-14 delivery of a GBU10/16/24, and the first use of night vision devices in combat. *Czerviski*

pounds! Meanwhile, the F-14As of VF-14 led strikes on the Afghan capital, Kabul, attacking a warning-and-target-acquisition radar as their sister squadron, VF-41, targeted an al-Qaeda training camp near Kandahar.

All totaled, nine Tomcat squadrons participated in OEF: VF-11 (F-14B), VF-14 (F-14A), VF-31 (F-14D), VF-41 (F-14A), VF-102 (F-14B), VF-103 (F-14B), VF-143 (F-14B), VF-211 (F-14A), and VF-213 (F-14D). More than 1,400,000 pounds of munitions were expended during OEF. VF-213 holds the distinction of delivering the first bombs of OEF, and on March 12, 2002, an F-14B, assigned to VF-11, delivered the first JDAM while flying a combat sortie.

On January 5, 1999, VF-213 Tomcats 163903 and 159619 engaged Iraqi MiG-23s and a lone MiG-25. Two AIM-54C Phoenix missiles were launched at the MiG-25, marking the first combat launch of this long-range missile by Navy Tomcats. No confirmed kills resulted from this engagement. *Author*

F-14A, 162698, flew combat sorties as the VF-14 "Tophatters" CAG during Operation Allied Force, OSW, and OEF. *Collens*

F-14A, 161274, a.k.a. "Betty," on November 9, 2001, following the final Tomcat cruise of the "Black Aces." During OEF, VF-41 routinely flew missions lasting six hours or more. In sixteen days of involvement, the squadron did not miss a single sortie, achieving a 100 percent mission completion rate. *Author*

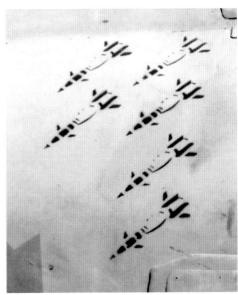

F-14A, 161295, assigned to VF-211 and photographed at NAS Oceana in August 2002, following a transfer from CVW-9 to CVW-1. During OEF, the squadron flew 2,100 combat hours and 850 combat sorties and delivered 41,000 pounds of ordnance. Sorties included CAS, CSAR, FAC(A), and TARPS. *Author*

F-14B, 161433, aboard the USS *John F. Kennedy* (CV-67) on July 31, 2002. An F-14B assigned to this squadron made the first combat delivery of a JDAM, on March 11, 2002. *Zweirko*

F-14B, 163225, photographed March 27, 2002, the day after the squadron's homecoming from OEF. During their final Tomcat cruise, the Diamondbacks flew 5,000 hours and dropped 420,000 pounds of ordnance, more than any other unit in CVW-1. *Author*

F-14B, 162918, VF-103, a.k.a. "San Antonio Rose," photographed May 23, 2002, three weeks before deploying to Operation Enduring Freedom. Following two combat tours in 2002 and 2004, it was retired to AMARC on January 5, 2005, and was scrapped there on March 12, 2008. *Author*

F-14D, 164600, VF-31, photographed May 5, 2003, returning from the 2002–03 OEF cruise in the northern Arabian Sea, Persian Gulf. This Tomcat was damaged in a landing accident at NAS Oceana and stricken on June 16, 2003. *Author*

F-14A, 158620, photographed February 16, 2002, landing at NAF Atsugi, Japan. On April 2, 2003, 158620 crashed in the Iraqi desert following a fuel transfer problem. *Hiroe*

F-14D, 164348, assigned to VF-213 and displaying forty-eight LGB symbols from OEF sorties. It was photographed during February 2002 at NAS Oceana. It returned to combat with VF-213 in 2005–06. It was delivered to AMARC on March 28, 2006, and was scrapped on July 21, 2009. *Author*

F-14A, 161603, VF-211, in April 2004. Note the Grand Slam tail markings, including the Battle "E," Safety "S," Precision Strike, and Admiral Clifton awards. Delivered to AMARC on August 17, 2004, this Tomcat was scrapped there on June 17, 2008. *Author*

Nine Tomcat squadrons flew combat missions during Operation Iraqi Freedom (OIF): VF-2 (F-14D), VF-11 (F-14B), VF-31 (F-14D), VF-32 (F-14B), VF-103 (F-14B), VF-143 (F-14B), VF-154 (F-14A), VF-211 (F-14A), and VF-213 (F-14D). This combined Tomcat force flew more than 2,500 combat-related sorties and delivered 1,452 GBU, JDAM, and Mk. 82 bombs. During OIF, the Tomcat reached its full potential and became a much-sought-after asset by ground troops who preferred its superior on-station and Forward Air Control capabilities.

Close-up of Operation Iraqi Freedom mission markings adorning F-14B, 163224, assigned to VF-32, June 2003. Of interest is the space shuttle nose art, a fitting tribute to *Columbia* (STS 107), which disintegrated on reentry, February 1, 2003. *Author*

F-14A 161276, assigned to VF-154, parked on the SARDIP ramp at NAS Oceana awaiting its ultimate fate, reclamation of reusable parts and equipment, followed by the destruction of the airframe. This Tomcat had departed NAF Atsugi, Japan, in September 2003. When I photographed it during January 2004, it had already been stricken from the Navy inventory. Of interest is the impressive Operation Iraqi Freedom scoreboard. The squadron flew 300 OIF combat sorties and delivered 320 tons of ordnance. *Author*

When F-14B, 163227, arrived at AMARC on April 20, 2005, it became the last "Red Ripper" Tomcat delivered to the "boneyard." On June 18, 2008, it was scrapped in place. "Red Ripper" Tomcats went out in style, contributing ten GBU-12s and 533 rounds of 20 mm ordnance to the war effort. During combat and training evolutions, the squadron delivered more than 110,000 pounds of live and inert ordnance, including GBU-31s. *Author*

F-14B, 162916, photographed during the final VF-32 Tomcat homecoming on April 17, 2005. This Tomcat was delivered on April 1, 1988, and served with VF-142, VF-143, VF-103, VF-102, and VF-32. This Tomcat made history on January 14, 2004, when it launched six AIM-54 Phoenix air-to-air missiles on a training flight. During Operation Iraqi Freedom, 162916 flew twenty-eight combat missions, delivering twenty-nine GBU-12s, one GBU-16, and five GBU-31, JDAMS. This Tomcat is currently on display at the Richard J. Gross *VFW Post*, 8896, East Berlin, Pennsylvania. *Author*

F-14B, 162918, assigned to VF-103, returning from the final Tomcat cruise of the "Jolly Rogers" on December 13, 2004. This Tomcat contributed two LGBs to the war effort during its final F-14 deployment. Retired to AMARC on January 5, 2005, and was scrapped there on March 12, 2008. *Author*

F-14B, 163220, assigned to VF-143 and photographed at NAS Oceana on January 14, 2004, less than a week before deploying to the Persian Gulf in support of OIF. This Tomcat was delivered to AMARC on March 17, 2005, and was scrapped by HVF West, Tucson, Arizona, on June 18, 2008. *Author / Van Winkle*

The old and the new: F-14D, 163894, of the "Bounty Hunters," next to its replacement F/A-18F, 165917, on the Oceana ramp on June 2, 2003. This "Bounty Hunter" Tomcat dropped forty-eight LGBs during OSW/OIF. Following service with VF-101, 163894 was SARDIP/Destroyed at Oceana on October 25, 2004. *Author*

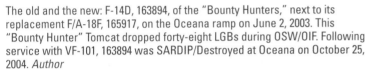

F-14D, 164602, on September 23, 2004. Blacklion 100 participated in OEF and OIF, as evidenced by the sortie totals superimposed on silhouettes of Afghanistan and Iraq. Delivered to the Navy on May 29, 1992, this Tomcat accumulated 4,558 flight hours, 1,290 catapult launches, and 1,296 arrested landings, including field arrestments. It arrived at AMARC on March 28, 2006. As we go to press, it is listed in storage there. *Author*

F-14D, 164601, photographed returning from VF-31's final WestPac cruise on October 31, 2004. Assigned to VF-101, it flew the final Tomcat air show demonstration on September 18, 2005. The following day it was flown to Castle Air Force and inducted into the museum there. *Author*

F-14D(R), 161163, VF-213, flying the "Stars and Stripes" during an OIF combat mission on December 10, 2005. The load-out consisted of a least one AIM-9 and an early example of the GBU-38 with a steel nose plug. Later examples used a barometric fuse. *USN/Kessel*

The final deployment and combat operations for the Tomcat involved VF-31 and VF-213, embarked aboard the USS *Theodore Roosevelt* (CVN-71) from September 1, 2005, to March 10, 2006. During this deployment, F-14D 161166 became the first Tomcat to utilize a new, off-the-shelf improvement known as ROVER. The system enabled the crew to see what the ground controller saw from his vantage point, eliminating the time-consuming effort of talking the crew onto the target. This new enhancement combined with the ability to deliver JDAMs significantly increased demand for F-14Ds throughout the combat zone. The last two Tomcat squadrons combined to deliver 9,500 pounds of munitions during 1,163 combat sorties and 6,876 flight hours. The final Tomcat combat mission was flown on February 8, 2006.

In the Persian Gulf on November 30, 2005, F-14D, 164603, assigned to VF-31, begins a climb-out in full afterburner after launching from the USS *Theodore Roosevelt* (CVN-71). During their final Tomcat deployment, VF-31 completed an unprecedented 1,606 combat sorties while flying 4,951 combat flight hours over Iraq. Upon returning stateside, the squadron was rewarded with the coveted CNO's Arleigh Burke Fleet Trophy and the CNAF Battle Efficiency Award. *Laird*

For decades, wives, family, and friends decorated the main gate of naval air stations to welcome home loved ones from a cruise. March 10, 2006, saw the return of Carrier Air Wing 8, CVW-8, to NAS Oceana, and the tradition was carried on in grand style. This sign was one of many welcoming home VF-31 and VF-213 at the completion of the Tomcat's final cruise.

CHAPTER 9

Tomcat Sunset

Although billed as a weeklong event at NAS Oceana during September 2006, the Tomcat Sunset began during May 2005, when VF-31 and VF-213 deployed to NAS Fallon for the final Tomcat predeployment detail. Carrier Air Wings deploy to Fallon and use its remote location, four bombing ranges, and excellent flying weather to integrate the various squadrons into a cohesive fighting unit. The wing then deployed to the Mediterranean and the Persian Gulf aboard the USS *Theodore Roosevelt* (CVN-71) on September 1, 2005, to begin the final cruise for the venerable Tomcat. *Potts*

Although billed as a weeklong event at NAS Oceana during September 2006, the Tomcat Sunset began during May 2005, when VF-31 and VF-213 deployed to NAS Fallon for the final Tomcat predeployment detail. Carrier Air Wings deployed to Fallon and used its remote location, four bombing ranges, and excellent flying weather to integrate the various squadrons into a cohesive fighting unit. The wing then deployed to the Mediterranean and the Persian Gulf aboard the USS *Theodore Roosevelt* (CVN-71) on September 1, 2005, to begin the final cruise for the venerable Tomcat.

The F-14's combat career ended February 8, 2006, at 1235 hours, when "Lion 204," F-14D(R), 161159, made the final Tomcat combat trap aboard the USS *Theodore Roosevelt* (CVN-71). The drawdown of F-14 Tomcats began more than a decade before the last combat trap. In January 1991, during Desert Storm, the US defeated one of the world's largest standing armies. The Soviet Union was in a state of collapse, and the catch phrase of the day was "Peace Dividend." As a result, defense spending was in decline and cuts were inevitable. In 1988, there were twenty-eight operational

Tomcat squadrons in service, including four assigned to Naval Reserve units. The two fleet replacement squadrons rounded that number out to an even thirty. By 1996, that number had fallen to twelve active, one reserve, and one fleet replacement squadron. Of the thirteen remaining Tomcat squadrons, one (VF-201) transitioned to the F/A-18A+ Hornet, and the remaining twelve to the F/A-18E or F Super Hornet. The first to convert were VF-14 and VF-41 following their 2001 OEF cruise, and the last two were VF-213 and VF-31, following their 2006 Persian Gulf cruise. Tomcats began to head to the "boneyard" known as AMARC, (later redesignated AMARC in 2007), Davis-Monthan AFB, Arizona, in increasing numbers. According to inventory data, nearly 200 Tomcats were interred there; only a handful returned to service. The Tomcat's nine lives were numbered. Those Tomcats not relegated to bake in the Arizona sun were SARDIPed in place. This military acronym stands for Stricken Aircraft Reclamation and Disposal Program. The process involved the removal of critical components and avionics. What was left was a hulk barely recognizable as an aircraft. The carcass was then cut apart, and its precious metals were recycled.

Beginning in the mid-1970s, Tomcat flight demonstrations were a mainstay at major air shows, especially those held at Naval Air Stations. The last official Tomcat flight demonstration drew Tomcat enthusiasts from around the world to NAS Oceana, Virginia Beach, Virginia, on September 16–18, 2005. Not only would the show feature the final Tomcat demo, but it would also mark the last public appearance of the F-14B, three of which, assigned to VF-32, took part in a simulated attack commonly referred to as a TAC Demo. The Swordsmen would be redesignated VFA-32 on November 5, 2005, transitioning to the F/A-18F. The "Grim Reapers" disestablishment ceremony was held September 15, 2005, a day before performing at the air show. The remaining US Tomcats, assigned to VF-31 and VF-213, were deployed to the Persian Gulf.

As previously mentioned, the last Tomcat trap following a combat mission took place February 8, 2006, and the last bomb was dropped from a Tomcat on the same mission. The final Tomcat homecoming from deployment took place March 10, 2006. A formation flyover preceded the recovery of both squadrons. The first to transition to the Super Hornet was VF-213, converting to the F/A-18F and designated VFA-213 on April 2, 2006. The

F-14D, 161159, assigned to VF-213, successfully trapped aboard the USS *Theodore Roosevelt* (CVN-71) on February 8, 2006, at 0035 hours, effectively ending the combat career of Grumman's iconic fighter. This particular Tomcat is now on display at the National Museum of Naval Aviation, Pensacola, Florida. *Foster*

On September 18, 2005, F-14D, 164601, performed the final official Tomcat demo at the NAS Oceana Air Show. The following day, 164601 was flown to Castle AFB and was inducted into the museum there. *Author*

"Christine," F-14DR-5, 159600, the oldest active Tomcat in the fleet at the time, lands at NAS Oceana on March 10, 2006, concluding the Tomcat's final deployment. Delivered as an F-14A on July 16, 1975, 159600 was upgraded to F-14D(R-5) standards, accumulating 6,008 flight hours, 1,614 catapult launches, and 1,614 arrested landings. Stricken on August 5, 2006, it was transported to Texas aboard a C-5 Galaxy and placed on display at the OV-10 Bronco Museum, Ft. Worth. *Author*

Blacklion F-14Ds on the Oceana ramp the day after the final Tomcat cruise on March 11, 2006. The colorful F-14D, 164602, is the squadron's "retro schemed" Tomcat. It was delivered to AMARC on March 28, 2006, and still resides there as we go to press. *Author*

LAST TIME, BABY...!

1976-2006

F-14 BLACKLION 30 YEARS

The last Tomcat catapult launch took place aboard the USS *Theodore Roosevelt* (CVN-71) on July 28, 2006. This historic event involved F-14D, 164341, assigned to VF-31. This Super Tomcat was delivered on July 18, 1991. It arrived at AMARC on September 20, 2006, where it was still resident as of this writing. *Laird*

F-14D, 164350, departing for permanent display at Palmdale, California. This Tomcat was delivered on February 7, 1992. It accumulated 4,809 flight hours, 1,322 catapult launches, and 1,334 arrested landings, including field arrestments. *Filmer*

F-14D, 163904, was selected to make the ceremonial final flight on September 22, 2006. Due to a mechanical issue, its place was taken by this Tomcat, F-14D, 163902. *Author*

"Tomcatters" of VF-31 would become the last Tomcat squadron and transitioned to the single-seat F/A-18E, officially designated VFA-31, on August 1, 2006; yes, two months before the final flight of the "Tomcatters."

The "official" Tomcat Sunset ceremony took place at NAS Oceana on September 22, 2006. More than 1,500 past and present Tomcat aviators, maintainers, and enthusiasts were on hand to bid farewell to the iconic Tomcat. To commemorate the Sunset, two VF-31 Tomcats were painted in a Tomcat farewell scheme, one in high-visibility markings (164350) and the other, 163904,

in low-visibility or tactic paint scheme. The latter was selected for a ceremonial flyby for those in attendance. Unfortunately, after taxiing out amid much pomp and circumstance, 163904 suffered a generator failure, and F-14D 163902 took its place and made a somewhat somber flyby, heading north and landing at nearby NAS Norfolk. The last cat standing, F-14D 164603, lifted off from Oceana's runway 23L at 0920 hours, October 4, 2006. It was flown to its birthplace, Bethpage, Long Island, New York, where it is currently displayed. Three nonairworthy F-14s remained at Oceana: F-14A 161151, the former FRAMP trainer; F-14B 162916, formerly flown by VF-32; and F-14D(R) 159600, previously assigned to VF-31. These departed by early 2008. BuNo 161151 is now on display at Tobyhanna Army Depot, Pennsylvania. BuNo 162916 is proudly displayed and cared for at the Richard R. Gross VFW Post 8896, East Berlin, Pennsylvania, and 159600 is cared for by the OV-10 Bronco Museum, Ft. Worth, Texas.

By October 4, 2006, F-14D, 164603, was the last cat standing. On that date, it was flown to its birthplace on Long Island, New York. When it touched down at Republic Airport, New York, 164603 had accumulated 4,436 flight hours, 1,282 catapult launches, and 1,296 arrested landings, including field arrestments. Officially stricken from the Navy rolls on September 28, 2006, it is proudly displayed in Bethpage, New York. *Author and LeBaron*

CHAPTER 10
The Last Cats Standing

Although Canada and Japan expressed interest in purchasing F-14 Tomcats, the only foreign operator was Iran. Following a study by the Imperial Iranian Air Force, it was determined that a de facto airborne early-warning radar system was required to cover Iran's vast and mountainous territory. During 1971, Grumman reached out to the shah, who already had shown interest in the F-14 Tomcat. A fly-off between the F-15 Eagle and F-14 Tomcat took place for the benefit of the shah and high-ranking Iranian officials during July 1973 at Andrews AFB. The event was a mere formality; the decision was already made. The Tomcat, AWG-9 radar, AIM-54 Phoenix, E-3 Sentry aircraft, and a new Westinghouse Air Defense System were precisely what the IIAF was in search of to defend its borders and fill gaps in their air defense radar net. An initial contract for thirty F-14s and 424 Phoenix missiles was signed late in 1973. On January 7, 1974, that order was increased to eighty Tomcats and 714 Phoenix missiles. The first Iranian aircrews reported to VF-124 for training during May 1974. No E-3s were delivered to Iran.

Although Canada and Japan expressed interest in purchasing F-14 Tomcats, the only foreign operator was Iran. Following a study by the Imperial Iranian Air Force (IIAF), it was determined that a de facto airborne early-warning radar system was required to cover Iran's vast and mountainous territory. During 1971, Grumman reached out to the shah, who already had shown interest in the F-14 Tomcat, 158623. A fly-off between the F-15 Eagle and F-14 Tomcat took place for the benefit of the shah and high-ranking Iranian officials on July 25, 1973, at Andrews AFB. The event was a mere formality; the decision was already made. The Tomcat, AWG-9 radar, AIM-54 Phoenix, E-3 Sentry aircraft and a new Westinghouse Air Defense System were precisely what IIAF was in search of to defend its borders and fill gaps in their air defense radar net. An initial contract for thirty F-14s, and 424 Phoenix missiles was signed late in 1973. On January 7, 1974, that order was increased to eighty Tomcats and 714 Phoenix missiles. The first Iranian aircrews reported to VF-124 for training during May 1974. No E-3s were delivered to Iran.

A total of seventy-nine F-14A Tomcats reached Iran before Shah Mohammad Reza Pahlavi was overthrown on February 11, 1979. The eightieth example, 160378, was undergoing modifications in the US and had yet to be delivered. It was embargoed and placed in storage at MASDC on May 20, 1981. Withdrawn from storage on September 23, 1986, it was reconstructed, modified, and pressed into service with PMTC, NAS Point Mugu, California. Tomcats received by Iran were not identical to their US Navy counterparts. Iranian Tomcats were not equipped with the AN/ARA-62 instrument landing system, KIT-1A, KIR-1A, KY-28 Secure Voice, and the AN/ALR-23 IRST system. The APX-81-M1E, (APX-82-A) IFF interrogator installed in Iranian Tomcats could interrogate only Soviet-designed aircraft. Phoenix missiles delivered to Iran had their ECCM suites downgraded, making them less effective if deployed against ECM suites aboard US aircraft.

Following the overthrow of the shah and the withdrawal of US and contractor support, Iran's Tomcat fleet languished, falling into disrepair. A handful of Iranian Tomcats were operational or in the process of being made operational in the weeks and days leading up to Iraq's invasion of Iran on September 22, 1980. If reports are correct, the first aerial victory scored by a Tomcat took place on September 7, 1980, when an Iranian Tomcat aircrew downed an Iraqi Mi-25 helicopter with its 20 mm cannon. According to authors Tom Cooper and Farzad Bishop, over 150 confirmed kills were achieved by Tomcat aircrews during the Iran-Iraq War, 1980–88.

It is difficult to estimate how many Iranian Tomcats remain in service or how many are mission capable. One thing is certain—F-14 Tomcats still patrol the skies over Iran.

F-14A, 160401, in US/Canadian markings. In 1977, the Canadian Department of National Defense considered purchasing F-14As to replace the aging CF-104s, CF-116s, and CF-101s. The deal fell through in 1978 due to high unit cost and skulduggery involving the government of Iran. *Lawson/NNAM*

The first Iranian Tomcat, 160299(H1), under construction at the Grumman facility. Improved Pratt & Whitney TF30-P-412A-powered Tomcats were delivered to Iran. *Grumman*

The last Iranian Tomcat in sand camouflage, F-14AM, 3-6049, was photographed at the International Iran Air Show in Kish, Iran, on November 17, 2016. *Filmer*

Former Iranian F-14A, 160378 (H-80). Embargoed and placed in storage at AMARC and then withdrawn from storage on September 23, 1986, it was overhauled and placed in US Navy service and assigned to the PMTC, Point Mugu, California. It was photographed in PMTC markings during October 1999. It returned to the boneyard on August 21, 2000, and was scrapped. *Robbins*

A pair of Imperial Iranian Air Force (IIAF) F-14A Tomcats in close formation during a training flight over Iran, March 1977. The Tomcat closest to the camera is 160306. During training missions such as this, the front seat was occupied by an Iranian pilot in training, and the rear seat, by an American flight instructor. *Davis*

The Imperial Iranian Air Force utilized a Boeing B707-3J9C as an aerial refueling platform. Iranian pilots, under the guidance of American flight instructors, are seen here learning the proper technique for aerial refueling using a hose and drogue. The Tomcat closest to the camera is 160342. *Davis*

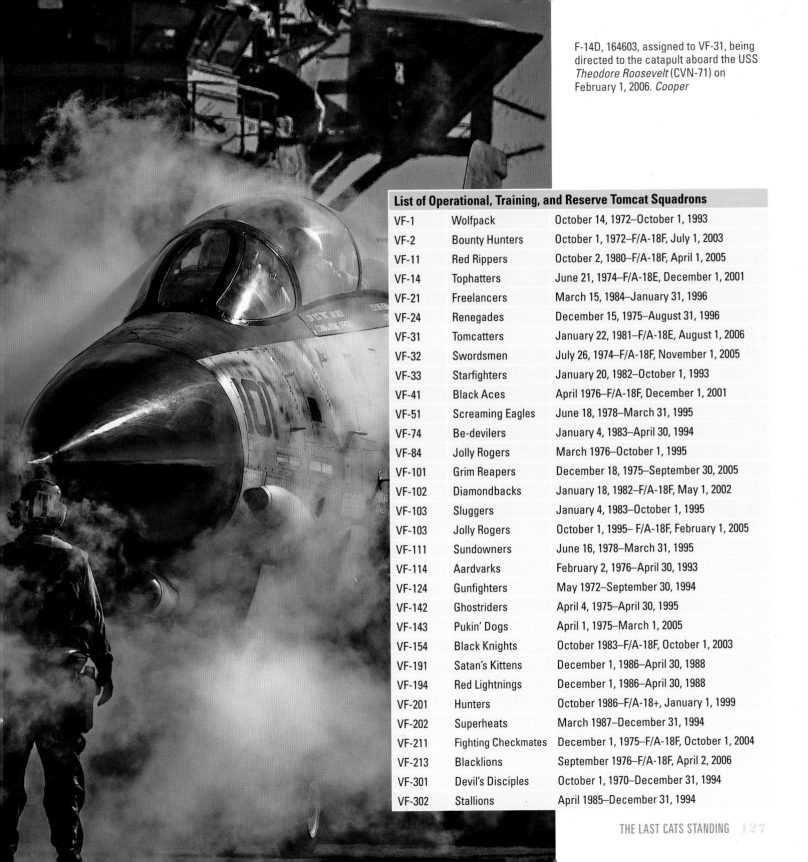

F-14D, 164603, assigned to VF-31, being directed to the catapult aboard the USS *Theodore Roosevelt* (CVN-71) on February 1, 2006. *Cooper*

List of Operational, Training, and Reserve Tomcat Squadrons

VF-1	Wolfpack	October 14, 1972–October 1, 1993
VF-2	Bounty Hunters	October 1, 1972–F/A-18F, July 1, 2003
VF-11	Red Rippers	October 2, 1980–F/A-18F, April 1, 2005
VF-14	Tophatters	June 21, 1974–F/A-18E, December 1, 2001
VF-21	Freelancers	March 15, 1984–January 31, 1996
VF-24	Renegades	December 15, 1975–August 31, 1996
VF-31	Tomcatters	January 22, 1981–F/A-18E, August 1, 2006
VF-32	Swordsmen	July 26, 1974–F/A-18F, November 1, 2005
VF-33	Starfighters	January 20, 1982–October 1, 1993
VF-41	Black Aces	April 1976–F/A-18F, December 1, 2001
VF-51	Screaming Eagles	June 18, 1978–March 31, 1995
VF-74	Be-devilers	January 4, 1983–April 30, 1994
VF-84	Jolly Rogers	March 1976–October 1, 1995
VF-101	Grim Reapers	December 18, 1975–September 30, 2005
VF-102	Diamondbacks	January 18, 1982–F/A-18F, May 1, 2002
VF-103	Sluggers	January 4, 1983–October 1, 1995
VF-103	Jolly Rogers	October 1, 1995– F/A-18F, February 1, 2005
VF-111	Sundowners	June 16, 1978–March 31, 1995
VF-114	Aardvarks	February 2, 1976–April 30, 1993
VF-124	Gunfighters	May 1972–September 30, 1994
VF-142	Ghostriders	April 4, 1975–April 30, 1995
VF-143	Pukin' Dogs	April 1, 1975–March 1, 2005
VF-154	Black Knights	October 1983–F/A-18F, October 1, 2003
VF-191	Satan's Kittens	December 1, 1986–April 30, 1988
VF-194	Red Lightnings	December 1, 1986–April 30, 1988
VF-201	Hunters	October 1986–F/A-18+, January 1, 1999
VF-202	Superheats	March 1987–December 31, 1994
VF-211	Fighting Checkmates	December 1, 1975–F/A-18F, October 1, 2004
VF-213	Blacklions	September 1976–F/A-18F, April 2, 2006
VF-301	Devil's Disciples	October 1, 1970–December 31, 1994
VF-302	Stallions	April 1985–December 31, 1994

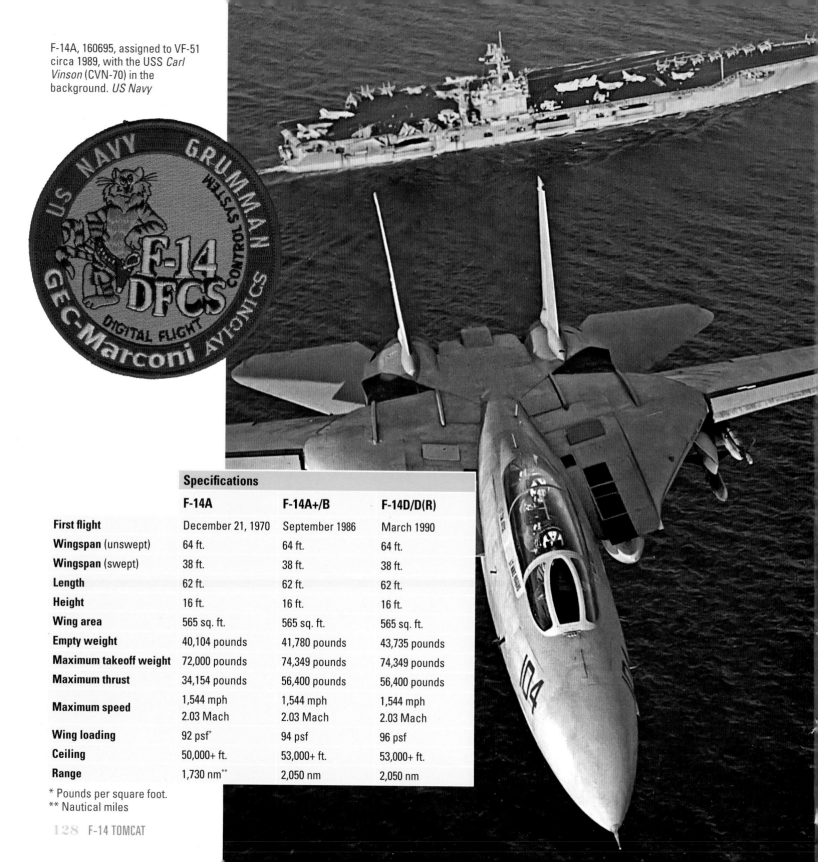

F-14A, 160695, assigned to VF-51 circa 1989, with the USS *Carl Vinson* (CVN-70) in the background. *US Navy*

Specifications

	F-14A	F-14A+/B	F-14D/D(R)
First flight	December 21, 1970	September 1986	March 1990
Wingspan (unswept)	64 ft.	64 ft.	64 ft.
Wingspan (swept)	38 ft.	38 ft.	38 ft.
Length	62 ft.	62 ft.	62 ft.
Height	16 ft.	16 ft.	16 ft.
Wing area	565 sq. ft.	565 sq. ft.	565 sq. ft.
Empty weight	40,104 pounds	41,780 pounds	43,735 pounds
Maximum takeoff weight	72,000 pounds	74,349 pounds	74,349 pounds
Maximum thrust	34,154 pounds	56,400 pounds	56,400 pounds
Maximum speed	1,544 mph 2.03 Mach	1,544 mph 2.03 Mach	1,544 mph 2.03 Mach
Wing loading	92 psf*	94 psf	96 psf
Ceiling	50,000+ ft.	53,000+ ft.	53,000+ ft.
Range	1,730 nm**	2,050 nm	2,050 nm

* Pounds per square foot.
** Nautical miles